Jeffrey Alexander and
Cultural Sociology

Jeffrey Alexander and Cultural Sociology

Jean-François Côté

polity

First published in English in 2023 by Polity Press

First published in French in 2021 as *La sociologie culturelle de Jeffrey C. Alexander* by Les Éditions Hermann in Paris and Presses de l'Université Laval in Québec

Polity Press
65 Bridge Street
Cambridge CB2 1UR, UK

Polity Press
111 River Street
Hoboken, NJ 07030, USA

ISBN-13: 978-1-5095-5555-0
ISBN-13: 978-1-5095-5556-7(pb)

A catalogue record for this book is available from the British Library.

Library of Congress Control Number: 2022949653

Typeset in 10.5 on 12 pt Sabon
by Fakenham Prepress Solutions, Fakenham, Norfolk NR21 8NL
Printed and bound in the UK by CPI Group (UK) Ltd, Croydon

The publisher has used its best endeavours to ensure that the URLs for external websites referred to in this book are correct and active at the time of going to press. However, the publisher has no responsibility for the websites and can make no guarantee that a site will remain live or that the content is or will remain appropriate.

Every effort has been made to trace all copyright holders, but if any have been overlooked the publisher will be pleased to include any necessary credits in any subsequent reprint or edition.

For further information on Polity, visit our website: politybooks.com

Contents

Preface

This book offers the first systematic and critical presentation of Jeffrey C. Alexander's cultural sociology. It was first published in French and was intended as an introduction to Alexander's sociological project, which remained little known in francophone sociology. This English version adds only small changes to the original French version. As Alexander's project in cultural sociology has now reached an international audience and is developing into a sociological movement that challenges the sociological discipline, it seemed timely to provide a systematic and critical overview of one of the most important sociologists of our time. Because Alexander's project in sociology aims at reforming the discipline, its scope and depth have to be understood both for how it internally developed and for what it proposes in terms of the analysis of contemporary society. As will be seen, these two traits converge in a reflexive commitment to promote the recognition and development of the *civil sphere*, a concept that Alexander patiently elaborated in order to highlight the possibilities of a democratic culture, deeply embedded in symbolic structures and practices. His sociological contribution is then accomplished by resituating the discipline within its active role in social life and is activated by a general interpretation that calls for hermeneutics in the reading of sociology and social life in general. There is little equivalent of such an ambitious and stimulating undertaking in sociology today.

This book was first initiated by discussions with Frédéric Vandenberghe, whose acquaintance with Alexander's sociology dates back more than thirty years. The writing was stimulated by discussions with Jeffrey C. Alexander himself, through encounters at international conferences and through a visit at the Center for Cultural Sociology at Yale University in the fall of 2019. For both their invaluable intellectual support and warm friendship, I want to thank Frédéric and Jeffrey, for whom sociology is as much a discipline as an occasion for developing stronger human relations. I also want to thank the two anonymous reviewers for their valuable suggestions, as well as Gordon Connell and Jeffrey Malecki for their help in making the text more readable in English.

Introduction

The renewal of sociology seems today perhaps even more urgent than ever. Whether it be the coherence of sociological analyses and theories from a strictly disciplinary point of view, the epistemological issues raised by the discipline with respect to its scientific claims, or even simply the relevance of sociological discourse to the great challenges of our time, questions about the status, value, and use of sociology are coming from all sides. Alain Caillé and Frédéric Vandenberghe have recently called for a refoundation of the discipline in the terms of a "new classical sociology," which they propose to consider in the light of the challenges of our time, suspended between the original expectations of the sociological project and its possibilities of development – beyond, of course, the professional advances it allows (Caillé and Vandenberghe 2016). It is in a direct echo to this call that the developments of Jeffrey C. Alexander's *cultural sociology* have long been situated, as he specifies himself. He has always been involved in an "anti-utilitarian" enterprise intended to refound a sociology resolutely centered on the analysis of culture (Alexander 2018b).

Cultural sociology has thus developed over the last twenty years in the United States and in the English-speaking world, with Alexander's work providing many of its predominant developments. Established at the Center for Cultural

Sociology (CCS) at Yale University, Alexander's cultural sociology is presented as a project to renew sociology as a whole. Today, it is promulgated primarily by two specialized journals, the *American Journal of Cultural Sociology* and *Cultural Sociology*, as well as a few more general edited works (Alexander, Jacobs, and Smith 2012; Hall et al. 2012; Inglis and Almila 2016), in addition to gathering a growing community of researchers around its project. Although it has not really crossed over into French, German, Italian, or Spanish sociology, mainly because of the lack of translations, cultural sociology undoubtedly appears as one of the most ambitious projects within the discipline at the beginning of the twenty-first century. This book intends to describe and analyze the project and achievements of cultural sociology by focusing on the contributions of its main theorist, Jeffrey C. Alexander.[1]

Alexander is one of the most important authors of contemporary sociology in the United States. His oeuvre, which now includes more than twenty books (and twenty-six edited or co-edited books), as well as dozens of book chapters and scholarly articles, stands out as a major contribution to sociology of all orientations. His work began with the monumental doctoral dissertation he completed at the University of California, Berkeley, in 1978 (and which is now published in four volumes (Alexander 1982a, 1982b, 1983a, 1983b), initially a critique of the last great theorist of American sociology, Talcott Parsons (1902–1979). Alexander's project was based on what he then called "neofunctionalism," but it changed in the middle of the 1980s as a result of a deeper reading of Durkheimian sociology, particularly *The Elementary Forms of Religious Life* (Durkheim [1912] 1963). Cultural sociology finds in this work many of its foundations and reference points, with the perspective of a new analysis of the question of *meaning* in sociology, relayed by a rereading of Weber, as well as a critique of Marx. However, Alexander marks this rereading of the classics with a concern for reflexivity – that is to say, a sociology that not only takes culture as an object, according to an "objective" analytical posture, but by means of analysis also actively participates in the constitution of culture itself.

The cultural sociology project was truly launched in 1998 with a programmatic article signed by Alexander and Philip Smith, his former student turned colleague at Yale University (Alexander and Smith 1998). This project presents a "strong program" in the sense given by the English sociologist of science David Bloor (1991): seeing science rooted in social influences and beliefs. Beyond this social constructionist perspective, there is also a question of ensuring that sociological theory not only includes axioms and concepts established in a rigorous manner, but that it is at all times supported by empirical studies capable of validating the theoretical framework that it proposes. Cultural sociology thus presents itself as a new way of considering sociology as a whole, even though its specific field of application is that of culture. Cultural sociology has since developed along lines that emphasize a pragmatics of meaning in terms of a semiology of dual oppositions, coupled with a "structural hermeneutics" applied to the study of cultural phenomena, which it considers mainly in terms of rituals, performances, and socio-political manifestations of the contemporary world, with an emphasis on their inscription in the *civil sphere*, an original concept that sums up much of its genuinely novel perspective (Alexander 2006).

Cultural sociology thus participates in the "cultural turn" that has taken place in sociology since the 1960s and 1970s with the rise of the Birmingham Centre for Contemporary Cultural Studies (Richard Hoggart, Stuart Hall). But its own project, while endorsing the problematic of the relative autonomy of culture as presented by Cultural Studies, radically dissociates itself from this by attempting to exceed the critical perspective inherited from Marxism which defined the latter's main orientation. The criticism of culture, in the eyes of cultural sociology, does not represent a sufficient method to develop a conclusive sociological analysis. It is in this context that Alexander also criticizes the sociology developed by Pierre Bourdieu, whom he reproaches for being unable to deal with the problem of domination (Alexander 1995: 128–202). Resolutely engaged in its efforts to contribute reflexively to the development of culture, cultural sociology intends to exceed the interpretations of the world and society that sociology has produced up to now.

By establishing itself as a new orientation of the socio-logical discipline, Alexander's cultural sociology raises several questions. Although it has produced innovative work in its treatment of cultural meaning – proposing to situate it in terms of ritualization processes, highlighting the perform-ative dimension of social action, recontextualizing the civil sphere beyond its Habermasian definition, or more recently presenting a vision of social life intended to counter cynical views of the political world – it is confronted with analytical, theoretical, and epistemological issues. Indeed, how far can we extend the reflexive scope of the analyses by short-circuiting the criticism we can make of them from a Bourdieusian or Marxist point of view? In what way is the theory proposed by cultural sociology likely to be confronted with other avenues of contemporary sociology, such as historical sociology, pragmatist sociology, or systemic sociology? Finally, is the structural hermeneutic approach that it puts at the forefront of its program compatible with the terms of a reflexive interpretation of contemporary culture or with the dialec-tical requirements that accompany it? It is these and other questions that this book proposes to answer in a critical examination of Alexander's cultural sociology.

In wanting to distinguish itself from the sociology of culture through a reflexive orientation (Alexander 1996a), cultural sociology employs its own participation to link theory and empirical research to affirm the symbolic functioning of contemporary society. It considers that the performative manifestations of the political world are to be analyzed for what they reveal of the ins and outs of political life in which the representation marks the climax. It is a matter not of questioning the forms of politicians' performativity in a mere critique of ideology but, on the contrary, of attending to the fact that, through these performances, the political world is led, political mobilizations can take place, and ultimately its aesthetic characteristics manage to impose themselves on the world. The credibility of these performances depends on their capacity to arouse debates on crucial issues for mass democracies, whether related to the presidential elections in the United States during the Obama era (Alexander 2010a, 2011a; Alexander and Jaworski 2014), the Arab Spring (Alexander 2011b), or even to the Iraq War or climate change

(Smith 2005; Smith and Howe 2015). This vision of politics – which refuses to question solely from the perspective of criticism, irony, or cynicism the value of those public manifestations whereby power puts itself on stage – voluntarily gives credibility to this functioning of our systems of political representation, while acknowledging the debt to the ways in which societies are structured by the civil sphere (Alexander 2012b).

Yet, it is not only "official" political manifestations that are the object of cultural sociology's analysis. The expressions of "minorities," insofar as they are expressed by the requirements of political representation, also show at a glance characteristics which indicate that resistance to power deploys performances where the autonomy of culture affirms itself. Thus, in the claims of African Americans, feminists, or the *déclassés*, and more so in the modes of expression these different minority groups put forward, cultural identities are formed by claiming their specificities. From a perspective similar to contemporary critical theory (Axel Honneth) and French pragmatic sociology (Boltanski, Thévenot), cultural sociology puts forward an analysis of social and cultural trauma that bears witness to the ways in which stigmatization is reversed and then channeled into political expression (Alexander 2012a; Alexander et al. 2004). Unlike these competitors, however, cultural sociology focuses not so much on the critique of power as on the power expressed in that critique from the horizons of the different minorities in our societies.

In the wake of its "strong program," cultural sociology has now extended its analytical reach to many phenomena, managing to gather a community of researchers inspired by its approach not only within the American Sociological Association in the United States and the British Sociological Association in England, which remain its main anchors, but throughout the English-speaking world and beyond (in Latin America in particular, as well as in Asia). From the arts to religion, from immigration to electoral campaigns, from the environment to the digital, the objects that attract its attention have multiplied in proportion to the interest it has aroused; from the problems of narration to those of semiotics and to those of interpretation, the epistemological, theoretical, and analytical issues it raises never cease to feed it and its developments. So much so that one could almost speak of the "cultural sociology movement" in the same way that one speaks of the "psychoanalytical movement" at the beginning of the twentieth century. In all of this, cultural sociology finds in Jeffrey Alexander – and in the sources of inspiration that motivated his work, such as Clifford Geertz or Robert N. Bellah – an eminent representative whose influence continues to grow. This is what we will discover in the chapters that follow. However, let us first situate the general context of Alexander's cultural sociology, as well as the view we can take of it.

The project of cultural sociology is one of "renovation," and it responds in several respects quite directly to the call for a "new classical sociology." It is by a direct rereading of the classics (in particular, Parsons and Durkheim, but also Marx and Weber) that Alexander proceeds first of all. He uses the advances of other disciplines (such as anthropology, with Clifford Geertz and Victor Turner, and semiology, with Roland Barthes), as well as other specific areas of study (in particular, cultural and performance studies, with Richard Schechner), integrating them into a more general theoretical perspective. Alexander also makes an epistemological shift in the aims of sociological analysis, situating it in a moment of reflexivity that is at one with social life, thus wanting to position himself away from objectivist visions that claim to be external to any particular point of view. Similarly, he emphasizes that the foundations of social life are not anchored empirically in a fundamentally utilitarian economic materialism but, rather, appeal to mechanisms of symbolic exchange, where a political world defined above all by issues of democratic representation and social justice takes shape. The three main lenses that guide the project of cultural sociology are thus the epistemological, theoretical, and empirical issues of sociological analysis. This does not mean, however, that its enterprise responds definitively to these issues.

Alexander returns to the debate between natural and cultural sciences, underlining the fundamental difference that Dilthey (2010) had already identified by placing "meaning" (rather than "things") at the heart of the analytical project of cultural (rather than natural) sciences (Alexander 2019). Interpretation thus takes over from explanation, the discovery of "laws" gives way to the recognition of the possibilities of generalization, and objectivity is relegated behind the subjectivity inherent in human practices. But doesn't this weaken the renewal of the sociological project from the start? Indeed, since Dilthey (as well as Weber, Rickert, Simmel, etc.), important milestones have been reached in the project of the sciences taking culture as an object; Ernst Cassirer's work, in particular, marked a crucial step in the capacity to situate symbolic forms as a "universal law" inherent to human expression in general (Cassirer 2000). Objectivity is then just a mode of objectification proper to any symbolic form, and it is thus merely human subjectivity that can claim this kind of relation to the world, whose universality is only acquired through an experience always open to modification. We recognize here the fundamental principle of any scientific theory, which is capable of being criticized and surpassed by another theory of a higher order. This position thus brings the natural and cultural sciences onto the same level: that of a mode of objectivation with a symbolic character where its plasticity emerges, showing how scientific theories themselves are animated by a capacity of self-transformation through a dialectical process while preserving their distinction of object.

The problematic of meaning, then, relative to the analytical approach of the sciences of culture, holds in fact to the nature of symbolic forms. Alexander's cultural sociology takes good note of this by orienting itself towards the seizure of cultural forms by the means of semiology, albeit according to the binary character of signification – a fundamental principle inherited from structuralism (associated with Saussurean linguistics, and even to Lévi-Strauss, as much as to Jakobson's understanding of message codification and to the literary approach of Barthes, as Alexander (2003) reminds us). In doing so, cultural sociology counts on a certain stability in its hermeneutics – that is to say, a possibility of association between the manifested meanings and their deep historical references, in particular during moments of political confrontation, which it also arranges in the orb of a binary opposition inherited from religion – particularly between the sacred and the profane. But, in doing so, does it not deprive itself of conceiving the *dialectical* character inherent in any symbolic form? Indeed, and especially from a historical point of view, it is striking to notice how the oppositions of former times are transformed to give birth to new oppositions; for example, if the category of "citizen," associated with the right to vote, during the early modern period was applied exclusively to male property owners (excluding women and peasants), the transformations associated with the mass democracies of the last two hundred years have gradually extended the same category of "citizen" to any individual. This means that the modern opposition between citizen and non-citizen has not only become (with all that it entailed in terms of "bourgeois morality" and the legal categories it supported) obsolete today, but it has been absorbed, in a dialectical reversal, into a new category that has dissolved the old opposition. This easy-to-grasp example is suggestive of others, perhaps less obvious at first sight, but which nevertheless structure social life and the moral universe through their transformations: witness the reversal of the typically modern relationship of domination over nature in the contemporary ecological register, or the legal provisions and moral judgments towards homosexuality developed from the second half of the twentieth century. These dialectical reversals show a dynamic at work in the symbolic world that is difficult to reduce to stable binary oppositions. Thus, it is the whole vision of the evolution of the world that seems to be translated not by the establishment of a static codification, but more by the constant overtaking and rearrangement of the symbolic order of our societies – even if, of course, strong elements of the social order, such as the regime of capitalist accumulation or certain traditional religious forms, apparently always resist changes (but is this really the case?). It remains enough to wonder about the capacity of cultural sociology to analyze, by means of what I would call a *dialectical hermeneutic* rather than a structural hermeneutic, such transformations. Cultural sociology cannot be satisfied with reaffirming the prevalence of a static social order but must manage to record the transformations of this order in the very analytical movement it produces. We find there the definition of its own reflexivity when it acquiesces precisely to the dialectical process that makes it sympathetic to symbolic forms and their intrinsic transformational movements.

Finally, this reflexivity, which obeys the socio-historical conditions of its time by adhering to a conception of science that it adapts to specific objects, corresponds to the cognitive, normative, and expressive place that cultural sociology takes today. But to do this, it must also recognize that its participation in the social and cultural order, resulting from the "relative autonomy" from which all symbolic expressions proceed, necessarily transforms the forms and structures of these symbolic expressions. In other words, cultural sociology – no more or less than all the other sciences – cannot be neutral, and it participates actively in the transformation of the social and cultural world, thereby finding a place within the contemporary political order. To what imperatives does this reflexivity within the sociological project respond? To what extent is it likely to lead to transformations beyond the analyses it produces? These questions remain on the current and future horizons of our societies. But this is definitely the challenge that Alexander takes up in the development of the project of cultural sociology – that is to say, the active contribution to shaping the contemporary symbolic world using analytical, theoretical, and epistemological methods. Let us therefore enter without further delay into the promising and exciting project that Alexander's cultural sociology offers us.

1

The "Strong Program" of Cultural Sociology

The project of cultural sociology was developed and took shape based on a short, relatively polemical text originally published in French in 1998, in which Jeffrey C. Alexander and Philip Smith laid the foundations of a "strong program" (Alexander and Smith 1998). They intended to subscribe to the vision of the sociology of science developed in the mid-1970s by David Bloor and Barry Barnes, whose fundamental principle is to consider that the *social* constitution of scientific knowledge is based on *beliefs*, and this is in accordance with elementary but strict – and strictly applied – principles.[1] The idea here was to distance "cultural sociology" as far as possible from a mere "sociology of culture," which was indeed defined in classical sociology (in the young Marx, the sociology of Max Weber, and the later Durkheim in *The Elementary Forms of Religious Life*, as well as the hermeneutic project of Wilhelm Dilthey), but which had never been able to find firmer reference points, as Alexander had made clear in his short piece on this specific issue (Alexander 1996a). This approach was furthermore downgraded in Parsons's sociology to the level of a static "cultural system" supported by "stable values," whose only variables able to escape the functional normativity fall into the category of "dysfunctions." The "strong program" of cultural sociology was then to free itself from these limitations and clear an original way for sociological analysis to illuminate cultural material in all its rich virtualities and possibilities.

In this desire to refound the analysis of culture along a well-defined programmatic axis, Alexander and Smith choose to compare cultural sociology to three other contemporary approaches, criticizing them for what they consider to be their axiomatic weaknesses. They consider first the approach of English Cultural Studies, arguing that it is in fact confined to an orientation which, while taking into account an analysis of *meaning* at the level of cultural codifications and textuality, only recapitulates the Marxist approach in the expressions of oppositional subcultures; for Alexander and Smith, Cultural Studies does not manage to assume a complete autonomy of culture, which thus remains always subjected to the conditions of domination within capitalist relations of power. Next, they consider Bourdieu, who leaves only a small place for creativity, assuming that culture in fact serves only "systems of stratification defined by class, and all that is important for dominant groups is to have their cultural codes embraced as legitimate" (Alexander and Smith, 2002: 141). This blockage, mainly linked to the concept of *habitus*, is in their eyes unable to adequately filter the conditions of cultural reproduction, thus leading to generalizations and a lack of attention paid to the active and versatile role of agents/actors. Finally, they address Foucault's approach, particularly the fact that the genealogical method he advocates in his early works (on hospitals, asylums, and prison environments) succeeds only in merging the terms of power and knowledge, preventing actors from having a critical grip on the understanding and interpretation of the symbolic and textual situations in which they evolve. In so doing, Foucault prevents himself from identifying the "rifts between culture and institutions" and ultimately locks himself into a determinism of structure from which even his later work cannot escape. We should note that the terms of these criticisms remain terse, dependent on the polemical framework in which they are expressed, and require further development and clarification – we will return to this in due course.[2]

The expression "cultural sociology," established in this way, had been used before, but in a more vague and clearly less committed way. Alexander had devoted two chapters in 1987 to examining, under the rubric of "cultural sociology," the "hermeneutical challenge" and the contribution of Clifford Geertz to such an approach (Alexander 1987: 281–329; Alexander 2008). Michèle Lamont and Robert Wuthnow (1990), in particular, had wanted to characterize the rise of the "cultural turn" in sociology by designating it as "cultural sociology," but this was largely a simple comparison between the American and European approaches in sociological studies on culture. Alexander himself, at that time (and in the same book as Lamont and Wuthnow) used the expression "cultural sociology" simply in reference to the recent creation, within the American Sociological Association, of a new section dedicated to this emerging discipline – while also pointing out the kinship between the aims of this new orientation and the advances of neofunctionalist sociology (Alexander and Colomy 1990) and introducing the binary model for analyzing the discourse of civil society which would become crucial to the whole enterprise of cultural sociology (Alexander 1992a).

Philip Smith also edited a book in 1998 whose title, *The New American Cultural Sociology*, suggests an intention to put the term "cultural sociology" on a formal footing. However, the chapters of this book are texts published previously by different authors who, while tackling the cultural question directly, did not subscribe to the principles of the "strong program" that Smith and Alexander were later to enunciate in their text. Smith announces, in a "pre-programmatic" way, the possibilities of cultural sociology by advancing the principles of a *middle-range* analysis targeting culture, social structures, and individuals as being co-implicated in the dynamics of meaning. He emphasizes in particular the "post-Parsonian" character of these developments and their resolutely empirical anchoring, anticipating that these possibilities could prove fruitful in the evolution of this tendency within the American sociological discipline. Thus, it is really with Alexander and Smith, but more specifically with the former, that the strongest impulse to launch the "strong program" of cultural sociology is to be found, because this program is based, in its later extensions, on the developments that Alexander himself has patiently put in place since the very beginnings of its sociological expression.[3] Let us turn briefly to these developments in order to follow the thread of this synthesis.

Alexander's "post-positivist" approach to sociology

The evolution of Alexander's sociological thought can be largely traced to the doctoral dissertation he completed at UC Berkeley in 1978, under the direction of Robert Bellah and Neil Smelser. The publication of this dissertation in a reworked form, entitled *Theoretical Logic in Sociology*, clearly forms the basic premise of the rest of Alexander's enterprise, particularly on the epistemological and theoretical levels. This four-volume work of more than 1,500 pages represents the first effort to rethink classical sociology in the terms that would lead, twenty years later, to the formulation of cultural sociology. I will concentrate in this chapter on the presentation of the epistemological aspect of this work, as well as the critique of Parsons's theoretical approach that it contains (in order to return later to the analyses of Marx, Durkheim, and Weber), since it is mainly from this work that neofunctionalism will be formulated, which arguably constitutes the touchstone of cultural sociology.

Alexander approaches the sociology of science from the point of view of the debates that have taken place about it in the twentieth century; his position is basically aimed at criticizing the positivism (of the Popperian type, rather than logical neopositivism) that has determined – and to a large degree continues to determine – the main positions in the natural and human (or cultural) sciences.[4] With this perspective, he bases his argument on the unsurpassable character of the relationship between theory and empiricism implied in scientific experience, underlining how the natural sciences tend to make the empirical the only criterion of validity for scientific knowledge, thus obliterating the theoretical view (and its general and metaphysical presuppositions). The human sciences on their side tend more often than not to imitate them in this respect in order to better assert their own scientificity. In a "post-positivist" perspective that he borrows from the critique of such a position – drawn mainly from the work of Michael Polanyi, Alexandre Koyré, Thomas Kuhn, Gerald Holton, and Imre Lakatos – Alexander thus proposes to base all scientificity on the recognition of the *relationship* between theory and empiricism. Moreover, he recognizes that the humanities, according to the very objects on which their analyses focus, have also tended to enter into the complex examination of the symbolic structures that present themselves within human reality – rather than seeing only the "object" that appears to the natural sciences in a way that is unproblematic (since appearing in its sheer "immediacy," it is unproblematized in the very operation that allows it to be isolated as an "object"). In other words, Alexander considers it practically inevitable that the human sciences are less precise in their analyses, because their objects are not only more complex but necessarily presented from the angle of the *relations of objectivation* that all human experience of the world contains, expressed in symbolic form according to very elaborate *structurations*.[5] This, among other things, is what, on the one hand, can create conflicts or confusion with regard to the "level" (of structuring) on which the analysis focuses and, on the other, calls for a "multidimensional" analysis. It allows the human sciences to formulate "generalizations," though not actual laws, within their theories, much like the natural sciences, without losing sight of the "specificity" or particularities of the objects linked to their empirical observations (Alexander 1982a: 34). This epistemological position is called "post-positivist," which serves as a foundation for the theoretical *logic* of sociology, on an equal footing with all the sciences by virtue of the specificity of its objects – and attached to the *meaning* conferred to these objects rather than to the objects themselves.

It is this epistemological position that allows Alexander to enter the debate concerning the discipline of sociology, and in particular its scientificity. Unlike Habermas, whose 1968 book *Knowledge and Human Interests* he quotes in places, Alexander does not recognize three orders of knowledge (positive, reflexive, and critical) and instead focuses his attention on the difficulties sociology has encountered since its origins in terms of its scientific foundation. He thus situates his position according to the capacity to join the general metaphysical presuppositions of all knowledge to the more specific objects to which the analyses relate on the empirical level, attempting never to lose sight of the multi-layered relationship that unites these two orders of things.[6] This conception of scientific knowledge is crucial, and it raises the question of its correct philosophical origins, in doubt because of the constant hesitation, in the development of sociology, between (neo-)Kantian and Hegelian philosophies. When he appeals, at the end of his first volume, to Hegelian dialectics to consider how sociological analysis can envisage concrete determinate negations in the relation between general and particular, arguing that theoretical logic must follow this model, Alexander illustrates the philosophical foundations to which sociology must resort in its own reflexive approach.[7] But, in doing so, it encounters important pitfalls, particularly the possible confusion between this general relation on the philosophical level and the other order of generality called "ideology" on the social level. Is it possible to distinguish the two, and consider the sociological enterprise as a space that analytically escapes the grip of ideology? Should we then discard the opposition between "facts" and "values," or that between "instrumental action" and "normative action" as basic referents of analysis?

Mannheim's (1954) sociology of knowledge had envisaged ideology, or "worldviews" (*Weltanschauungen*), as unsurpassable in the understanding not only of social reality but of scientific activity itself. Alexander contests this proposal, pointing out that it goes against any possibility of situating sociological analysis non-ideologically, and that it destroys, moreover, any possible position for a post-positivist approach by annihilating the scientific value of general presuppositions with respect to knowledge that is not strictly linked to empirical truth (Alexander 1982a: 39–46). The efforts to circumvent this problem, whether of a methodological, empirical, or modeling nature, coming from different areas of sociology and from different levels of its practice, have not succeeded in establishing a logical "generality" according to which the sociological enterprise can find its fundamental definition and its adequate justification, apart from ideology.[8] For Alexander, only in the recognition of the multidimensionality of the logic inherent in sociology can this problem be solved. Indeed, some of the classical oppositions of the sociological discipline, such as that of the fundamental epistemological subject–object relationship, or the opposition between idealism and materialism, or between voluntarism and determinism, must be considered for what they are: oppositions that cannot be dissolved but that must simply be assumed, and then overcome. Thus, in the case of the analysis of social action, for example, this must be considered according to its two sides (subjectively voluntary and determined by the social order). For Alexander, the reference model in this context remains Talcott Parsons's *The Structure of Social Action* (1968), in which Parsons reread and synthesized the classics of sociology (especially Weber and Durkheim, in addition to Pareto and the economist Alfred Marshall). But, as we will soon see, even this effort at theoretical synthesis by Parsons failed, according to Alexander, because of the incompleteness of his epistemological positioning, which confused on the analytical level the questions of social order and individual action, in addition reducing the whole analysis by orienting it on the strictly normative level (Alexander 1982a: 196–7, n. 97). However, this criticism, which will in fact give rise to Alexander's neofunctionalist enterprise, remains within the framework elaborated by Parsons in *The Structure of Social Action*, and it is along this axis that the whole theoretical logic will be oriented.

Indeed, Alexander envisages a confrontation of sociological theory primarily in terms of the two problems that Parsons had outlined at the outset of his rereading and recomposition of classical sociology (Pareto, Weber, and Durkheim). Parsons identified the problem of *social order* as fundamentally what should preoccupy sociology in terms of understanding, interpreting, and explaining individual action. In his critique of utilitarianism, Parsons was primarily concerned with showing that social order cannot simply correspond to the supposedly "rationalizing" aims of Scottish and English Enlightenment philosophy, from Locke and Hume to Bentham and John Stuart Mill, because of their ignorance of the composition of a social order brought to light by Hobbes, whose *Leviathan* ([1651] 2006) poses as the inescapable presence of the State in the regulation of individual actions. For Parsons, who recognizes that utilitarianism has become the central reference of a society whose evolution is reduced to classical political economy (he instead favors the position of marginalist economics in Marshall (1890), which he integrates into his new sociological synthesis),[9] the solution was to recognize individual social action as structurally associated with social order. Such social order is defined according to a logic that can be recomposed from the foundations of the discipline, as long as we keep our eyes fixed not on the antinomies it has produced (collective consciousness in Durkheim, and the individual meaning attributed to action in Weber) but, rather, on the synthesis that can be drawn from them. Alexander thus follows Parsons quite closely as he restates these two questions in relation to contemporary developments in sociology, which allows him to criticize a good number of approaches – from symbolic interactionism (Blumer 1969) and ethnomethodology (Garfinkel 1967) to phenomenology (Schütz 1967) – that have lost sight of the role of social order. On the other hand, Parsons's extensions into systemism and its successors, found in the very criticisms made by Blau (1975) and Coleman (1960), disregard the specifically individual determinations that deviate from a simple reproduction of the social order, whether expressed empirically or defined theoretically.[10] In both cases, Alexander argues that it is because of the confusion of the levels of analysis – as well as the reduction of analyses to either individualistic or collectivistic, idealist or materialist presuppositions, where rationalism is usually asserted as the ultimate social norm, and where action is reduced to its instrumental character – that the project of sociology remains burdened with insurmountable problems. Because of this, he argues that theoretical logic must be defined according to three main principles that will allow him to refound sociology in a post-positivist framework: *first*, an objective evaluation that passes through a universal reference to the structures of action and social order; *second*, an objective evaluation that recognizes the autonomy of both action and social order according to a synthetic perspective; *third*, and finally, an objective evaluation of action and social order according to a multi-dimensional approach capable of exercising a hierarchical judgment of the levels involved in the analysis (Alexander

1982a: 113–26). These three principles govern the theoretical logic at this moment, which becomes the engine of a "post-positivist" epistemological position, and which engages the reformulation of the project of sociology. This reformulation goes through a rereading of classical sociology (Marx, Durkheim and Weber), which are the object of volumes 2 and 3 of *Theoretical Logic in Sociology*; it is by way of reading, criticizing, and synthesizing this classical sociology elaborated by Parsons that Alexander proceeds in the development of his own argument. It is therefore necessary to understand his position in relation to Parsons, which becomes decisive not only for establishing the initial project of the neofunctionalist sociology proposed by Alexander in the first half of the 1980s but also for understanding the inflection he will then make towards Durkheimian sociology and Cultural Studies in the second half of the decade, finally leading in the late 1990s to the formulation of cultural sociology itself.

From Parsons to neofunctionalism

Alexander's reading of Parsons, in volume 4 of *Theoretical Logic in Sociology* (the most extensive of the four), is certainly critical, but this criticism is not so radical as to completely overturn functionalism (or structural functionalism). The proposed term "neofunctionalism" shows quite well what it is about: reforming, through a more assured epistemological position, Parsonian sociological theory beyond both Parsons's followers and his critics (Alexander 1983b: 1–7). The main advantage that Alexander sees in Parsonian sociology is its multidimensional character, which it deploys analytically. Indeed, Parsons was not content simply to identify the opposition between individualism and collectivism but proposed a synthesis, first in terms of the concepts of *systems of action* and *action frame of reference*, which are defined in relation to the social dispositions offered to the individual and the capacities of observation that concern them. These concepts are then elaborated in the differentiation offered by their distribution among various subsystems of action (namely the biological system, the personality system, the social system, and the cultural system, plus their reciprocal interactions and respective integrations).[11] It is through this multidimensionality that sociology can truly claim to have a more complete analytical grasp of the complexity of social reality.

Parsons's presence as a leading theorist in twentieth-century sociology, as well as the influence generated by this theorization (in the United States, of course, but just as much in Europe),[12] makes his thought important not only for anyone interested in the history of the discipline but also for its present evolution and its future possibilities. Alexander thus situates Parsons as the point of arrival of classical sociology, through the synthesis carried out at the end of the 1930s, and the point of departure of contemporary sociology, proposing a grasp of the structure of social action and the more complete developments of post-war systematization. However, throughout all this, Parsons insists on "integration," which remains problematic; while modern societies have acted in the direction of "differentiation" of their areas of practice (a characteristic already established by Herbert Spencer but reinforced analytically by Durkheim) by conferring on different institutions and individuals an autonomy of practice (in the economic, political, juridical, cultural domains), the contrary demand of "integration" has also been enacted, but in a more problematic way. This is what is shown, for example, by the anomic character of the social order, as Durkheim sees it, or by the permanent state of crisis in which society apparently finds itself. The sociological problem par excellence being, in Parsons's eyes, that of the social order, it is a question for him of conceptualizing the way in which individual action, once differentiated according to the areas of practice of modern society, can subsequently be reintegrated into this order. Parsons captures very well the way in which relations between institutions achieve this integration, not only by developing subsystemic relations of autonomy and exchange but by assuming a higher level of integration. This occurs first within the social system, perceived as integrating the different subsystems of action (organism and personality), then beyond this within the cultural system, allowing "values" to be organized in such a way that the configurational variables (*pattern variables*) offered to individuals allow them an overall integration into the various subsystems of action. The personality system, as an individual subsystem of organization underlying this set of functional relations, is thus considered from the point of view of its capacity to establish relations to the other subsystems of action (through different media such as money, influence, power, etc.) in an overall structuring which corresponds to the cultural aims established in the values. The famous organization of AGIL (*adaptation, goal attainment, integration, latency*), proposed by Parsons in *The Social System* (1951), allows us to grasp the composite and complex set of operations required in the integration of individual action into the social order.[13] It is the synthesis reached by this organization of AGIL that will be the object of Alexander's main criticism of Parsons, whom he will reproach for having reduced the understanding of motives for social action in favor of its normative integration within the social system, itself frozen in a cultural system with stable "values." As he puts it: "By so undermining the analytic autonomy of the subjective element, the multidimensional aspect of order is lost" (Alexander 1983b: 24). Moreover, and because of Parsons's insistence on this element of normative integration, Alexander also criticizes him for being able to view social order only in terms of the equilibrium that must prevail within each system and subsystem of action, since this equilibrium (eventually called "homeostatic," in the cybernetic extensions of Parsonian theory) is a sine qua non for their existence and survival, or maintenance.[14] Neofunctionalism is rooted in this critique of Parsons, a critique which, while valid, still contains enough confidence in the Parsonian synthesis that it should not be fundamentally questioned; rather, it should be reformed to offer more fruitful analytical developments – in particular from the point of view of empirical analyses based on multidimensionality (Alexander 1983b: 279).

These developments are announced in an article by Alexander and Paul Colomy, where the programmatic character of neofunctionalism is outlined, particularly with reference to the critical extensions of Parsons offered by his functionalist colleague Shmuel N. Eisenstadt. These extensions are essentially fourfold: "an emphasis on process and innovation, on the role and significance of interests, the omnipresence of conflict, and the disruptive aspects of culture" (Alexander and Colomy 1985: 12). In other words, Eisenstadt allows Parsonian functionalism to break out of the narrow rut of functional normativity, considering – especially through a rereading of Marx (on conflict) and Weber (on the individualization of meaning) – how the functionalist perspective can be enriched by expanding its analytical possibilities. Here, the role of cultural models promoted by different groups in political struggle for power and resource mobilization (symbolic and material), where these groups can develop interests and visions of the overall social order of different orientations in relation to the prevailing order, becomes an axis for capturing the social dynamics at work on an historical level. This leads to a more refined theorization of institutionalization, as well as a more articulated view of the relationship between the social system, culture, and the (re)definition of the social order. These are all elements that Alexander will use in his promotion of neofunction-alism. What he will retain, fundamentally, is the concept that societies rely on contingencies at the level of solidarity relations, power, and distribution of goods (ibid.: 14), which, from the point of view of its analytical possibilities, will translate for Alexander into a greater openness towards a reformed functionalism.[15]

If the program of neofunctionalism is well founded, it is because it is committed to deepening the analytical links and theoretical requirements that can complete the advances of Parsonian systematization, notably on the side of symbolic interactionism (Herbert Blumer), collective behavior (Ralph Turner), and the processes of institutionalization, mobilization, contestation, and transformation of the social order (Alexander and Colomy 1985: 16–21). These elements will be part of not only the principles of neofunctionalism but also cultural sociology, which is indeed the result of all these theoretical recompositions allowing Alexander to attain the multidimensional analysis he had identified as fundamental to his "post-positivist" approach. The work leading to the analytical refinement, envisaged both theoretically and empirically – for these two are also always intertwined – was spread out over a long period, during which there was much hesitation about its name. From neofunctionalism to cultural sociology, there were still, from the mid-1980s to the late 1990s, several directions that Alexander took, ranging from the search for a new synthesis between macro- and micro-sociological approaches, studies into meaning, the definitive "cultural turn" based on a rereading of Durkheimian sociology, and even a Cultural Studies approach.[16]

Following these advances we can see how neofunctionalism definitively transformed into cultural sociology. By leaving aside the name of neofunctionalism in favor of cultural sociology, Alexander does not so much disavow the roots of his approach as specify the object on which it will henceforth focus. After situating neofunctionalism in the tradition of Parsons, thus making it a classic of the sociological discipline, it was a question for Alexander of seeing how to reorganize sociological analysis according to the unsolved problems of Parsonian systematization (Alexander 1998b: 12, 210–33). In the first place is the micro and macro link in sociology, rejected by Parsons in favor of normative integration but problematized in a new way by the approaches of symbolic interactionism and ethnomethodology, which must themselves be resituated in a framework that allows for the apprehension of not only inter-individual but social relations more broadly. This amounts to consolidating the recognition of the Parsonian division between "personality system" and "cultural system" mediated by the "social system" – considered from now on as a medium of interactions not only from the point of view of the normative integration inside the institutions of social life.[17] "Structures" therefore do exist at this level, but they are constituted by symbolic codifications that are much more flexible than the simple "media" identified by Parsons and determined by the empirical capacity of actors and agents to form and transform meanings.[18] This implies that culture cannot be presented only from the point of view of values established in a stable way through a general reading (theoretical, according to observation, but also normative, according to a choice and a reduction) of social life, and that one must recognize in it a more profound autonomy, a plasticity, of which structural functionalism did not manage to decipher either the extent or the importance in relation to its own analytical aims (Alexander 1998b: 216–21). Secondly, the meeting place par excellence of this analysis must be circumscribed by the *civil sphere*, which becomes in some way the substitute of the "social system" and which, through its dynamics of exchanges, meetings, conflicts and agonistic struggles, presents itself as the real center of social life and of cultural life in action. It will also serve as the basis for all the *drama* that will arise in the heart of cultural sociology analysis, once the two analytical corollaries of the civil sphere have been set up: those "dramatic meanings" – that is, symbolic actions will be apprehended either in "pragmatic" terms, as the "performances" of the social actors, or in media narratives. This new theoretical synthesis will be that of cultural sociology, once the strict framework of neofunctionalism is overcome. The stages that will lead to it include the passage by Durkheim, resolutely engaging the object of "culture," then the transition to a position that makes the analysis of this object not a mere sociology of culture but a *cultural sociology* (Alexander 1988a, 1992a, 2003). This project is gradually developed not only through rereading, criticism, and synthesis but also by organizing the desired analytical perspective.

From neofunctionalism to cultural sociology

The synthesis presented by cultural sociology, beyond the statement of its "strong program" of 1998, was to be constituted at the turn of the twentieth and twenty-first centuries on very broad bases, going first to the creation of the Center for Cultural Sociology at Yale in 2002[19] and then to the foundation of the journal *Cultural Sociology* in England in 2007 and the *American Journal of Cultural Sociology* in 2013. There has been a proliferation of works along these lines, notably within the American Sociological Association and the British Sociological Association, including the *Oxford Handbook of Cultural Sociology*, a voluminous work of more than 800 pages that brings together the contributions of many duly accredited "cultural sociologists" (Alexander, Jacobs, and Smith 2012; Hall et al. 2012; Inglis and Almila 2016). Having reached this point, where it was a question of consolidating a certain analytical orthodoxy beyond rival approaches (even in the field of cultural sociology itself),

Alexander and his colleagues do not hesitate to speak of this enterprise as the establishment of a "church" – rather than a sect – and thus of a true school of thought.[20] Pursuing this objective by establishing authority in the field, cultural sociology has also attempted to foster internal debates around what has become of this field of study, aiming to avoid undue dispersion by concentrating points of tension that may become valuable analytical stakes: the relations between structure and event, model and variations, solidarity and hierarchy, discourse and materiality, daily life and public ritual, interpretation, explanation, and analytical validity (Alexander, Jacobs, and Smith 2012: 12–22). Twenty years after its programmatic arrival, cultural sociology has not only found its footing but, because of its wide scope and collaborative ramifications in the academic field, has become a true sociological phenomenon. At the heart of its activity are the definitions of symbolic action and cultural order, which are the two strong concepts from which the analytical enterprise on the sociological level can unfold.

Of course, such advances in sociology raise their share of criticism. From the beginning of his "post-positivist" enterprise, Alexander was criticized, on the one hand, for the terse, if not arbitrary, character of his criticisms of other approaches and authors and, on the other, for the difficulty, if not opacity, of the positions he defended with respect to his own program.[21] Criticism did not disappear over time, and the "strong program" of cultural sociology also gave rise to questions, in particular on the very debatable character of its relation to criticism (and to critical theory, as first developed by Adorno and Horkheimer, and subsequently by Habermas).[22] Nevertheless, and as they testify by looking back on the first decade of its existence, the "strong program" of cultural sociology remains promisingly ambitious in its reformulation of the theoretical questions that have marked the human sciences, from psychology to history, through philosophy and anthropology (Alexander and Smith 1998, 2002). These developments are still ongoing, notably touching on the analytical fields of performance, politics within the civil sphere, the theory of social trauma, and iconicity as a primordial dimension of cultural existence. And finally, if there is a fundamental principle to be retained from the point of view of the analytical enterprise, it is that of the recognition of the autonomy of culture, to which cultural sociology intends to contribute in a reflexive and decisive way – that is, by recognizing and foregrounding its own contribution to contemporary cultural development. It is there that we find, in my opinion, the crux of the whole enterprise.

A new analysis of the relative autonomy of culture based on reflexivity

Cultural sociology emerged in a particularly stark way, mainly under the influence of Robert Bellah and Clifford Geertz and through a rereading of Durkheim, offering to "post-positivist" epistemology and sociological theory an expressive synthesis between the relative autonomy of culture and analytical reflexivity.[23] The autonomy of culture means here that symbolic forms are not determined by economy, politics, technology, or other structures that escape subjective will, although the cultural symbols certainly interact with each of these domains. As Alexander (1990: 2) writes: "Culture is the 'order' corresponding to meaningful action," and, in this sense, "[s]ubjective, anti-mechanistic order is conceived of as followed for voluntary reasons rather than because of necessity in the mechanistic, objective sense."[24] Thus cultural sociology understands itself fundamentally through "the idea that any action, no matter how instrumental, reflexive, or coerced vis-à-vis its external environments, is embedded to some extent in a horizon of affect and meaning," by seizing the capacity for "reproduction and transformation of the structure" to reach the "ideal foundation" of institutions (Alexander and Smith 2002: 136). Applied to itself, in its sociological analytical practice, this idea enables cultural sociology to participate in cultural evolution without therefore being attached to, or in fact ever attempting to claim, the simple status of neutral observer of social life with an objectivist scientistic character.

This is perhaps what most clearly differentiates cultural sociology from a mere "sociology of culture." Alexander put forward this position in the short text calling for a "strong program," emphasizing that the requirement of reflexivity gave cultural sociology the duty of establishing itself as a strong alternative to the mainstream program of sociology as a whole. Because of the objectivity claimed by sociology in its aim to be scientific (thus reducing culture to the simple rank of "object" like any other), sociology is apparently always situated exterior to the object and requires contextualization to explain truly cultural determinations (Alexander 1996a). But culture cannot simply be the result of "context"; it is above all a "text," and the analysis of these texts engages sociology hermeneutically. This position was gradually developed by Alexander, notably by taking into account the Durkheimian sociology of cultural phenomena (anchored in the study of religious phenomena), as well as the approach taken by Weber and an engagement with anthropology – of which Clifford Geertz gives the best example in his attempt to define the social universe in terms of the symbolic structures that compose it. However, according to Alexander, the latter fails to offer anything other than an interpretation which allows for the description of symbolic activities, always bound to the simple contingency of their manifestations, and thus cannot take the place of a symbolic order possessing its own virtualities, both hermeneutic and sociological.[25] Rather, a cultural sociology properly speaking must go further, affirming its capacity to "discover, by the interpretative act, what these informing codes and narratives [of culture] are" (ibid.: 3).

This impulse will come to motivate the methodological orientation of cultural sociology in a radius that goes from semiotics to hermeneutics, via pragmatics. Many strands are involved here, mainly a rereading of the sociological tradition according to this reflexive perspective, plus an innovative coupling of structuralism and the hermeneutical program of the "sciences of the mind" (*Geisteswissenschaften*), with the contrasting positions of poststructuralism and postmodernism – each of these classical or contemporary approaches will be re-evaluated, criticized, and surpassed by the "strong program" of cultural sociology. In a sense, one could grasp this whole exercise from the point of view of the intense dialectic imposed by theoretical logic, starting from the "post-positivist" position discussed above; however, in my opinion there are a few noteworthy obstacles in the way.

First of all, the symbolic forms and the structures to which they give rise (as much in institutions as in discourses or individual action) are related not to their own (dialectic) virtualities but to the relations established between actors and institutions. In a sense, this returns the approach to a Kantian or neo-Kantian dualism in which the question of the foundation of subjectivity (and its arbitrariness, even) again becomes problematic. Since the developments of Hegelian philosophy and its criticism of the Kantian position, a displacement of the foundation of this subjectivity has indeed taken place, shifting to the level not of the individual but of symbolic mediation itself (or the "Concept," if we want to stay with Hegelian terminology). In this form of idealism, the wider concept of freedom, rather than the individual subjective will, is most important (on the social as well as the historical level) (Hegel 1991). The dialectical virtuality of this mediation means that individual subjectivity undergoes the test of a dual signification, which it is not entirely able to do (since it is inherent to the symbolic mediation embodying meaning itself in a dialectical fashion), but with regard to which it is always situated. Ernst Cassirer (2000) has re-examined this aspect, posing the existence of symbolic forms as the necessary order that all human society faces, which becomes the dilemma of a historical evolution torn by the opposition between union and division (this represents for him the internal dynamics of any symbol). This situation, lived in a more or less conscious way in the history of societies (though usually displaced to the level of mythical or religious symbolic representations that make divine will an unattainable extra-human reality), is exacerbated in the contemporary context where the human origin and destination of symbols (in language) and symbolic structures embodied on the socio-historical level (in institutions) are recognized. This suggests an obligation to recognize their formation as well as their transformation, not only "formally" (i.e. in relation to the evolution of symbolic forms) but also "substantially" (i.e. in relation to the possibilities that these symbolic forms offer to the concrete development of social life).[26] Thus, for example, the ideal of freedom which had animated the development of modernity was replaced in the nineteenth century by an ideal centered more on equality. To what extent does cultural sociology manage to recognize this ideal and situate it within the symbolic transformations taking place in our societies? How does it manage to grasp this "ideal foundation" at the heart of contemporary institutions and the social struggles being waged today?

In a sense, it is indeed a mission for cultural sociology to reach the reconstruction of the contemporary moral order from the point of view of culture. However, this path implies an historical return likely to retrospectively enlighten the analytical possibilities offered to us today from the concrete symbolic structures accessible to us. Thus, if Hegel, in *The Elements of the Philosophy of Right* (which can perhaps be considered the first sociological treatise because of its treatment of what he calls the "objective spirit," its systematic analysis of the categories of social life, as well as the respective relations that compose it), had managed to make this exercise within the framework of the historical development of Reason, the later evolution of thought, from Marx to Weber and beyond, indicted the ultimate achievement of modernity.[27] Indeed, de Tocqueville ([1835] 2004) had already noticed, in the immediate aftermath of Hegel, that, within the mass democracies succeeding bourgeois democracies, it became more difficult to change morals than to change laws. Because of the very dynamics of legislative efforts in the aftermath of modernity's institutionalization, it was necessary to illuminate the functioning of morals (or what de Tocqueville called "habits of the heart" and "habits of the mind"). Therefore, the foundations of legislative activity had to be able to recognize themselves in a "civil religion" capable of cementing the overall orientations of society.[28] This required research into the foundations of culture, and thus a hermeneutics – albeit with a dialectic character. It had to show symbolic transformations at work, expressed in the "limited" character of symbolic structures, not only on the social and historical planes but in its own participation in these transformations.[29] An excellent example in this respect is given to us by Marcel Mauss (1989), in his short text on the *person*: a preeminent symbol of modern societies, especially when associated with the new norms of isonomy gradually put in place from the first third of the nineteenth century, whose origin and destination seem unequivocal and tied to the views of political equality as a project of contemporary society.[30] To what extent can cultural sociology surrender to this kind of exercise? This is what we will discover in the next chapter as we explore Alexander's rereading of the sociological tradition, beginning with Durkheim.

2
A Rereading of Durkheim: Social Ritual and Cultural Significance

Alexander's rereading of Durkheim is central to the whole development of cultural sociology, constituting the initial pivot between neofunctionalism and the studies of culture that follow from the second half of the 1980s, gradually adding more precision to the latter. Durkheim appears first of all to Alexander as an essential step in the development of classical sociology, and so the second volume of *Theoretical Logic in Sociology* is devoted to him, in a discussion shared with a rereading of Marx.[1] It is also in this volume that Alexander introduces a clarification of what will become a "double hermeneutic" within his theoretical logic. By a ricochet of his cultural sociology, the first hermeneutic concerns the interpretation of the classics of sociology and the second concerns the interpretation of social life (Alexander 1982b: 1–7). Whereas the first volume of *Theoretical Logic in Sociology* had served mainly to establish his epistemological position, this second volume (and the two subsequent ones) put forward more specific theoretical orientations by interpreting the classics of sociology with the aim of reactivating their heuristic potential. This obviously works through criticism, particularly of their analytical presuppositions, but it also goes beyond them while acknowledging their limits, which is always useful when recontextualizing the body of a new analytical project. It is thus a question of taking note of the historical distance that separates us from the classics by pointing out aspects of their approaches that stumble because of contingencies and/or errors situated on the historical level, but also by offering innovative analytical possibilities if the rereading allows us to grasp limitations in the "state of mind" of their authors (ibid.: 374–6, n. 17). The hermeneutic that affects the classical texts of sociology is important because it constitutes, for Alexander, the very nature of the project of the humanities. This project must be articulated in the absence of a consensus concerning the foundations of the discipline and its formation. It must also be articulated around the recovery of insights frozen in texts that are socio-historically dated (thus corresponding to questions and problems of their time), as well as the issues (situating their scientific value and scope) that always remain present in the sociological enterprise. The other side of hermeneutics, the analysis and interpretation of social life, appears as the possible result of this rereading in relation to the questions and problems that run through contemporary social life, and thus focuses on specific empirical findings that feed the analytical project.

Alexander's book *Durkheimian Sociology: Cultural Studies* (1988a) does just that.[2] The book includes a general presentation and interpretation of Durkheimian sociology, as well as a series of more empirical analytical applications by Alexander and other contributors. The overall position builds on Durkheim's sociology of religion (which Alexander comes to refer to as "religious sociology"), focusing on the issues that the writings of the late 1890s began to (re)dramatize. It is only at this moment, Alexander writes, that Durkheim's "cultural program" truly emerges, because he is in possession of a theory of the symbolic processes linked to religious phenomena, allowing him to undertake a reading of contemporary social phenomena in light of their classifications – particularly that which appears in the distinction between the sacred and the profane (1988a: 2–3). If the most remarkable case in point remains the publication of *Les formes élémentaires de la vie religieuse* (1912), Alexander points out that it is the more recent publication of the studies carried out by Durkheim in the second half of the 1890s, as well as his very first writings from the 1880s, which already contain the most assured workings of his approach. This allowed him to take up again with fresh vigor the question of the moral foundation of the social order, according to a perspective that grasps the "internal dynamics of symbolic and ritual systems" (ibid.: 5). These are the elements that will become central to cultural sociology, even if it will also want to distance itself from them in a style close to the philosophical anthropology that emerged from *The Elementary Forms of Religious Life*.[3] Let us see how Alexander sets them up and deploys them in the framework of his own empirical analyses.

The presence of the religious in cultural life

Alexander's interpretation of Durkheim's work, contrary to what is usually perceived, is that it is best seen not so much as positivist as a hermeneutic of social life. Indeed, Alexander perceives a proximity between Dilthey's enterprise and Durkheim's (at least, in his last period), but suggests that Durkheim allows for advancements in concrete analysis, contrary to the hermeneutical tradition which has often been content with a statement of principle that does not lead to specific and empirical interpretations of culture (Alexander 1988a: 16, n. 7).[4] To get an idea of the deep motivations of Durkheim's sociological enterprise, however, one has to go back to his very first writings, which echo both the biographical imprint left by the context and events of his training and the seeds of the argument he was developing in relation to questions of action and order within a European society that was then undergoing a major transformation. Rejecting the idea that society could be based on a utilitarian logic, as promoted by the prevailing political economy, and rejecting a socialist state government of an authoritarian nature as advocated by the more radical left, in the mid-1880s (i.e. before he became a professor at the University of Bordeaux), Durkheim tried to develop a perspective in which the voluntary character of action was combined with the capacity to integrate into the social order. While he rejected symbolic mediation as sufficient to ensure the sought-after social cohesion, he instead first opted for feelings of sympathy and then the recognition of "habits" as the source of an adequate social morality (Alexander 1982b: 75–118). For Alexander, it is indeed morality (and the search for the social foundations of such a morality) that is at stake in Durkheim's sociological research. Durkheim's work would manage to account for the necessity of voluntary adhesion of individual action to the social order on the basis of a motivation of an affective or emotional nature, rather than a utilitarian one (a way of marking an "irrational" opposition to economistic rationalism as a motivational basis for action). If the Durkheim commonly remembered by the sociological tradition is above all that of the "great analytical completions" with a positivist flavor – the one who in the 1890s produced *On the Division of Social Labor* (1893), *The Rules of Sociological Method* (1895) and *Suicide* (1897) – by interpreting the initial foundations of the project in the very first writings, and then by linking them to later writings, the true Durkheim is revealed (see particularly Alexander 1986a, 1986b). The most significant place to find this Durkheim is of course *The Elementary Forms of Religious Life* of 1912, but this work systematizes a reflection that had been going on for nearly twenty years, revolving around the understanding of the place of religion within human society – which concludes that society reveals itself fundamentally in its religious manifestations. The moment of this realization came, by Durkheim's own admission, in the course on the history of religion he taught in Bordeaux in 1894–5, as well as through his reading of Robertson Smith on the history of religions, and then in his 1899 article on the definition of religious phenomena, which constituted a fundamental reorientation of his sociological project (Alexander 1982b: 235–42).[5] It is at the point where religion is defined according to its essentially social nature, the social being then defined as essentially religious, and where the "sacred" character of certain cultural forms appears, that a set of practices and meanings are determined which structure the whole of social existence in a simple "profane" dimension, resulting in an irreducible binary opposition (sacred/profane). Through a finely conducted analysis, Alexander argues that Durkheim's entire intellectual project actually culminates in his later writings, where he reveals the details of the kind of sociological enterprise he had been nurturing since the 1880s – and which will serve as an initial reference model for Alexander's cultural sociology itself.

The secularization of religion that Durkheim puts forward corresponds to the requirement of modernity, which consists of managing to explain rationally what society has produced more or less consciously, but which then becomes essential for understanding social cohesion. Morality, if it can have a scientific definition, has much to learn from what religion has shown to be an effective social force, since it is the *raison d'être* of societies: their "being together." The sacred, which is shown to be at the heart of human cultures, structures the social universe in its opposition to the profane, and it is thus a question for Durkheim of seeing how one manages to preserve this constitutive principle of the social order by seeing it at work at the heart of individual action. Here we see a translation into rational terms of what previously could not be explained, since its foundation was divine and by definition escaped human understanding. In other words, Alexander insists on locating in Durkheim a shift that, beyond modernity and its rationalist scorn for religion, provides a space of refoundation for the religious at the heart of societies (Alexander 1982b: 242–50). Durkheim expressed himself clearly on these points by noting in particular how in modern history, following the development of rationalization, revolutionary moments took on a religious, even sacred, character. Events such as the Reformation and the Renaissance, bourgeois revolutions, and even the revolutionary undertakings of the nineteenth-century socialists, take on their true meaning only as effervescent social experiences where the "collective feeling" was animated and spread, literally creating social transformations which produced new forms of meaning and expressed a religious allure – thus reworking the constitutive opposition between the sacred and profane.[6] Once this redefinition of the "sacred" with rational sociological content had been established, Durkheim put forward three concepts that became fundamental in Alexander's eyes: ritual, authority, and representation (Alexander 1982b: 244). Ritual accounts for a voluntary action where the feeling of participation in the social order prevails, based on feelings and affects that create an adhesion to a common figure (a

god) and to other individuals (the community). Authority is
expressed through an ambivalence which makes it is as much
feared as respected, as much disputed as desired, resulting in
a constraint not simply external but also interiorized on the
individual level. Representation situates an externalization of
the meanings which are consequently internalized, as structures of social life, comprised of affective, normative, and
cognitive dimensions. According to Alexander, by carrying
out this series of redefinitions, Durkheim succeeds in establishing not merely a simple sociology of religion but a *religious
sociology*, in the sense that it accomplishes a reflexive analysis
that succeeds in not only extracting meaning and significance
from social life in terms of religion but also reciprocating in
the form of a sociologically founded morality that takes up
the principles of the religious (Alexander 1986a, 1986b). By
shedding light on the importance of the religious element
within social life, Durkheim commits himself to a program
of cultural analysis capable of recognizing that religion goes
far beyond the economic and even political structures of
social organization, according to goals that transcend these
horizons. And while Durkheim himself may not be prepared
to explicitly recognize the role of religion in reorienting his
own program – as Alexander points out – he nevertheless
becomes a crucial source of inspiration for thinking about
the autonomy of cultural phenomena, and hence the project
of cultural sociology.

Alexander gives examples in which Durkheim pushes his
understanding of the religious sources of morality that flow
into the heart of symbolic conceptions of contemporary
society, showing not only how individualism but also the
family, the state, and the law are repositories of prominent
symbols that structure social organization, just as religion did
in the context of traditional and modern societies (Alexander
1982b: 263–79). If the expression of individualism manages,
according to Durkheim, to correspond to the dispositions of
individual action while meeting the requirements of the social
order, it is because individualism has become a symbol of
contemporary society, that it has acquired within the latter a
"sacred" destination, and that it thus corresponds symbolically to the very structures of this society. As a symbol, it
crosses social communication, reaching individual interiority

as much as the exteriority of expressions and practices, thus situating its "transcendent" position in relation to social existence. Durkheim thus manages, in his sociology of religion, to reaffirm the importance of symbolic representations through social structures, according to the model that religion has bequeathed to societies.

Paradoxically, however, this interpretation of Durkheim has not been confirmed by subsequent sociologists. Parsons's reading of it suffers from a reduction and assimilation to the normative order incapable of giving it this prominence, and even the works of Durkheim's immediate successors (Mauss, Fauconnet, Halbwachs, etc.) in the school he founded did not sufficiently grasp the importance of religion in the history of sociology. That is, according to Alexander, they did not sufficiently grasp the importance of this *religious sociology*. Alexander's interpretation of Durkheim is thus radical in the sense that it seeks to highlight an interpretation of his sociology that has been overlooked – except perhaps in the advances of the Collège de sociologie (in Roger Caillois and Georges Bataille, in particular).

According to Alexander, even Marcel Mauss, undoubtedly Durkheim's closest collaborator, failed to renew the project of an analysis of social life on its religious basis, even though Mauss anchored his orientation in an anthropological perspective where a clearly hermeneutical horizon emerges. In the article that Durkheim and Mauss co-signed in 1903 (Durkheim and Mauss 1963) on primitive forms of classification, the key idea that will be developed in *The Elementary Forms of Religious Life* is already present: that the symbolic forms of representations recorded in the life of traditional religions are directly related to social organization and appear to be linked in their substantial content to the structures of the social order – the prime example being totemism, as was later analyzed by Durkheim. If this is true for traditional societies, it is equally true for contemporary society, except that one must consider that the transformation of symbolic forms, particularly in the scientific domain, also corresponds to structures of contemporary social organization. Mauss partially follows this path when – in the wake of Durkheim's recognition of the "sacred" character of individualism in contemporary society, which has today become a prominent symbol of social organization – he returns to the socio-historical development of the *person*. He shows how, from its archaic origins in Roman theater and law, then through Christianity, and up to the philosophical development of bourgeois European modernity, this symbolic category asserts itself more and more on the social level (Mauss 1989). However, in other studies such as *The Gift* (2000), Mauss does not manage, according to Alexander, to seize the same ideas as Durkheim by relating symbolic representations to social structures; he instead withdraws to the material conditions of empirical practices (Alexander 1982b: 310–13).

Taking these positions in reverse, the theorization proposed by Alexander returns to the sources of Durkheim's sociology, offering an analysis of social life in which the religious can be given the place it deserves. This, however, is possible only by showing that Durkheim failed to a certain extent to push his *religious sociology* to its full potential. There was an inability to show how the "profane" dimension of existence (such as within the economy, politics, or instrumental action in general) can only ever be structured by the "sacred" dimension, and how also the idealism of his position towards religion must be confronted with the materialism of existence, thus reinforcing the theory on the level of empirical demonstration (Alexander 1982b: 292–6). Two examples drawn from the empirical analyses proposed by Alexander in the wake of this return to Durkheim will illustrate how he does this, extending Durkheimian analyses into contemporary contexts, while at the same time paving the way for the cultural sociology project gradually taking shape.

A sociology of religion in social life: politics and technology

The first of these examples is drawn from an analysis of the Watergate affair, the scandal that marred American politics in the 1970s and led to the resignation of President Nixon – a unique event for the American presidential institution. In his article on this issue – "Culture and Political Crisis: 'Watergate' and Durkheimian Sociology" (1988b) – Alexander attempts to apply the principles he drew from

his rereading of Durkheim to a contemporary event. The
challenge of this analysis is to show how the whole affair
had taken on the consistency of a religious ritual, through
which the institution of the presidency, defined as "sacred,"
had first been tainted ("polluted," writes Alexander), and
then eventually "purified" in the course of the journalistic
investigation relayed by the Senate Committee. Throughout
the whole affair, not only with Nixon's resignation but also
in its aftermath, Alexander locates a ritual significance that
first endangered and then regenerated political morality in
the United States.[7] This symbolic dramatization was illustrated in particular by a journey – assiduously followed in
public opinion, in particular in the televised hearings of the
Senate Committee – of an ultimately agonistic nature, where
the opposition between "good" and "evil" saw "good"
triumphing, thus restoring the "sacred" aura to the institution
of the presidency. The elements that Alexander invokes to
mark his analysis stem from a dynamic in which social actors
(the president, journalists, senators, the public, citizens, etc.)
are considered not only by the functionality of the roles
they assume in social organization but by the deep symbolic
resonance that these roles have within the political morality
associated with the presidential institution. As the institution
par excellence through which social organization is defined
in the United States, the presidency occupies a central place
in political life, distinguished particularly insofar as it relates
to the difference between "sacred" and "profane" activities,
while obviously locating the continuity between the two. In
fact, routine political activities ("profane" in this sense), such
as those of exercising the right to vote, publicly expressing
one's opinion, taking an interest in politics, and the like, are
only understandable from the point of view in which political
institutions (the Congress, with the House of Representatives
and the Senate, the Supreme Court, and the presidency
– which structure the *triumvirate of* power) appear to be
"sacred." The burglary at the Watergate Hotel in Washington
on June 17, 1972 – for the purpose of spying on members of
the Democratic Party to benefit the Republican Party during
the presidential election campaign that would bring President
Richard Nixon back to power (in November of the same
year) – appears at first glance to be a simple "profane" action

with no link to the institutional "sacred." However, due to the careful investigation by the *Washington Post* journalists Bob Woodward and Carl Bernstein, under the guidance of an informant ("Deep Throat," who we eventually learned was in fact Mark Felt, assistant director of the FBI), the Senate Committee was established and conducted a political investigation. It was demonstrated that President Nixon not only knew about the embezzlement but even ordered it – thus committing an illegal activity – illustrating a true "desecration" of the supreme political institution of the executive branch. Alexander follows the details of this case closely, "recodifying" in a religious register what initially appeared to be a mere political scandal. He does this because, in his eyes, what is at stake in this context is the *political morality* of the central institution of the United States.[8] With great detail, Alexander rereads and interprets this event through the deep symbolic structures that it mobilizes, going as far as to show how a parallel emerges between the prose-cutor (Archibald Cox) and Protestant morality, reaching then American "civil religion," and creating the context that would tip public opinion from a relatively benign judgment to the perception of fault that must be publicly atoned for. In this hermeneutic framework, "good" and "evil" confront each other in a binary opposition that the investigations (both journalistic and senatorial) exposed, showing that the president, incarnation of the "good," had in fact sided with "evil." The shift in public opinion occurs not only in the semiotic register but also in the moral register, through a televised ritual closely followed by the American public (and thus the electorate), which served as a re-enactment of public confession as it was practiced in the Protestant (if not Puritan) religious world. The resignation of President Nixon on August 9, 1974, a precedent in American political history, served as the denouement of a political and moral crisis that had shaken the institution of the presidency to its roots – as well as the entire institution of American political power. Once this religious ritual had been accomplished in the symbolic structures of American culture, political morality could be restored, and the "sacred" could take its rightful place at the center of American social life. This is the vision that emerges from an application of Durkheim's religious sociology in the analysis of a contemporary political phenomenon. Alexander shows in this way how the religious always acts within social life through the mobilization of its principal categories: ritual, the "sacred"/"profane" opposition, the division between "good" and "evil," and the authority of political morality.

Another example of the way in which Alexander interprets the presence of the religious in contemporary social life is provided by the reading he makes of that purely "technical" object (at least in appearance), the computer, that "information machine." By proceeding to the analytical examination of a corpus of texts, between the years 1944 and 1984, when the computer was presented to the public by various magazines (popular and scientific), he shows that this object, which one could not imagine to be more "profane," had come to develop in reality a "sacred" signification. His chapter "The Sacred and Profane Information Machine" in *The Meanings of Social Life* shows that the qualifiers one associates with this machine, from its initial development full of promises of "salvation" until its gradual generalization to a use in daily life that takes on the contrary color of "damnation," cannot be interpreted otherwise than through recourse to the vocabulary of religious codification (Alexander 2003: 179–92). Here, again, the confrontation between "good" and "evil" serves as a backdrop to the structural hermeneutic, which reminds us that the profane is always tied to the sacred world, in spite of all the appearances of (post)modernity, and that religious sentiment leads moral judgment in daily activities, as long as we know how to see beyond their more or less innocuous façade. Technology, the prime symbol of rationalization and instrumental activity, is thus not devoid of religious or even "sacred" connotations, since it represents, and is represented by, a whole symbolic heritage. This is important because, for Alexander, it is "[o]nly by understanding the omnipresent shaping of technological consciousness by discourse [that we] can ... hope to gain control over technology in its material form" (ibid.: 192).

Several things are to be retained from these two examples, for they will not only be important in the development of cultural sociology but will also raise epistemological,

theoretical, and analytical questions. First of all, we see
how the binary oppositions (sacred/profane, good/evil, etc.)
become a deep analytical reference, capable of anchoring a
semiotic categorization within the structure of the symbolic
expressions of social life. These are not simply identified
and pinned down but are also codified according to their
oppositions and their dynamics.[9] However, on this level, we
can already see that the dialectic of symbolic forms enables
their presentation according to and overcoming structural
opposition. This explains the reversal of polarization, or
the inversion of polarity, of which they can episodically be
the object, especially in the creation of new forms that this
opposition allows in their dialectical overcoming – that is
to say, in their transformations. So the oppositions are not
really situated on the definitional level.[10] In other words, it is
not the dialectical virtuality of symbolic forms that is implemented in their location and their movements. However,
the recourse to structural linguistics, in Saussure's case, and
up to a certain point in Lévi-Strauss's structuralism, does
allow for a linking of symbolic expressions to structures,
but without the repositioning of structures being called into
question. This is apparent in the relatively "static" interpretation of the Watergate affair, where it is a question of
restoring political morality, beyond or below the important
transformations that were affecting American political life at
that time (the new power acquired by the media, the relative
disaffection with politics by the electorate, the permanence
and prevalence of the reference to Watergate in subsequent
presidencies through the suffix "-gate" associated with other
presidential scandals, etc.).[11] This methodological disposition
that plays on binary oppositions in a static fashion thus has
a theoretical incidence, which has to do precisely with the
possibilities of "religious sociology" to stand as the horizon,
so to speak, of cultural sociology, if not sociology *tout court*.
That one is able to recognize the religious underpinnings
of symbolic forms should not prevent one from admitting
that their transformations – according to the requirements
of political life, science, or philosophy – make possible the
emergence of new virtualities and analytical possibilities, and
this is because the symbolic structures themselves are thus
transformed.[12] Finally, on the epistemological level, the place

of the dialectic, not only in relation to the foundation of the symbolic forms themselves but as a disposition of analytical reflexivity, must also be recognized as part of the sociological project. At least, this is what can be agreed upon from the moment one accepts that cultural sociology participates actively not only in the consolidation of the social order but in its active transformation. It is with these precautions in mind that we pursue developments in cultural sociology, particularly in relation to Durkheim's importance for Alexander's project and his later developments in this regard, including his rereading of some of advances in pragmatism he wants to include.[13] For the moment, however, let us remain on this terrain of a cultural sociology tied to Durkheim's "religious sociology" and its analytical consequences.

Symbolic forms of meaning in contemporary society

The development of Alexander's analytical program reached a definitive stage in the late 1990s, as we saw in the previous chapter, with the expression of the "strong program." This program is primarily concerned with enabling analytical advances that link theory and empirical practice together. The demand for this is found in the recognition of symbolic expressions and structures, the model of which, for Alexander, is to be found in the late sociology of Durkheim. But the consequences of this orientation, rooted in a Durkheimian "religious sociology," go so far as to call into question subjects of great significance: to what extent can the analysis of contemporary society reveal this almost direct association with the religious universe? Doesn't politics intervene as an instance of symbolic representation fundamentally different from religion? Must modernity, which was – in appearance at least – understood as a forceful opposition to religious tradition, be finally recognized as only a smokescreen with respect to the deeper pursuit of a structuring of the world, which cannot escape the mythical foundations of religions – and of the religious? Such interrogations inhabit, in an important way, contemporary hermeneutical reflection.[14]

Alexander's cultural sociology confronts these questions without shying away from the debates they bring about. Analyzed from this position, contemporary political discourses, such as those that feed the rhetoric of the "war against terrorism," appeal – whether they like it or not, or, better, whether they *know* it or not – to deep symbolic structures that remain mostly hidden from view but that are nevertheless linked to expressions that renew them. They are, in a way, "habits of meaning," or sedimentations of meaning in relatively stable structures, which are mobilized to make decisions in agonistic contexts (as we have seen in the case of Watergate, or in the more ambivalent case of computer technology). The task of cultural sociology is based on this idea of understanding, by means of a hermeneutic interpretation, the connection of these forms of language to the deep structures that give rise to them: this is what its "structural hermeneutics" is about. The task, in other words, is "to bring the unconscious cultural structures that regulate society into the light of the mind," a task approaching "a kind of social psychoanalysis" that allows an investigation of "the social unconscious" in order to "reveal to men and women the myths that link them so that they can make new myths in turn" (Alexander 2003: 3–4). This hermeneutic perspective appeals to these unconscious structures, or to this misunderstanding in the representations and expressions that we believe we control, but whose foundations usually escape us. But it cannot be a "hermeneutics of suspicion," as Paul Ricœur (1965) named it in reference to Nietzsche, Marx, and Freud. Influenced by Ricœur, who promotes the precedence of narratives in the organization of social life, Alexander's cultural sociology certainly does not wish to position itself as a simple critical endeavor, denouncing the alienation of which social actors are victims or the reification of the structures of power that are involved in domination (economic, political, or cultural), as we will see in the next chapter. Cultural sociology insists instead on recognizing that "collective emotions and ideas are central to its methods and theories precisely because it is such subjective and internal feelings that so often seem to rule the world, ... [s]ocially constructed subjectivity forms the will of collectivities, ... shapes the rules of organizations, ... defines the moral substance of law,

[and] provides the meaning and motivation for technologies, economies, and military machines" (Alexander 2003: 5).

From this we understand that the main future orientations of cultural sociology will deepen the symbolic dimensions of social life (such as ritual, performance, morality and its authority, or politics in general) on the basis of the following observation: "In our postmodern world, factual statements and fictional narratives are densely interwoven" (Alexander 2003: 5), and that the binary nature of symbolic codification (sacred/profane, good/evil, true/false) is inherent to them. However, it is not simply a matter of celebrating the presence of symbolic structures and their discursive and pernicious effects, for "only if cultural structures are understood in their full complexity and nuance can the true power and persistence of violence, domination, exclusion, and degradation be realistically understood" (ibid.: 7).

The program of cultural sociology is thus complex and very broad, and not without ambiguities either. If it recognizes the range of symbolic structures in their relation to everyday expression, it also grants them a "sacred" value in the measure of their power to shape the practices to which they are related. The transformations that can appear at this level, if they manage to cause changes in social codifications, do not manage to restructure or reconstruct the symbolic foundations on which they rest. Finally, if it is possible to consider elements of criticism in relation to the effects of violence, domination, exclusion, and degradation by understanding their sources, then this criticism does not rely on a "hermeneutics of suspicion." The foundations of the analysis being thus laid down, the theoretical and empirical program of cultural sociology can be pursued. In a continuation of Durkheim's attachment to the virtualities of ritual, Alexander turns to the anthropology of Victor Turner, who makes the link between ritual and theater (or dramaturgy), as well as to Clifford Geertz, who patiently tries to decipher the "web of meanings" and deep symbolic structures through which all action is linked, and to which one has access through a "thick description."[15]

This theoretical program is guided by two objectives: continuing to reread the canon of classical sociology and nourishing this rereading with contributions from new theoretical horizons developed in contemporary sociology, anthropology, semiotics, hermeneutics, and other emerging disciplines such as performance studies. In his relationship to classical sociological theory, Alexander encounters, beyond Durkheim, Weber's sociology of religion, especially in its relationship to the fate of modernity. But, before this, Alexander confronts that other critic of religion: Marx. Indeed, it is in relation to Marx that cultural sociology is going to pitch its "critique of the critique," arguing that Marxian critical theory does not manage to reach the aims of a theoretical logic likely to correspond to the true expectations of contemporary sociology. So let us turn now to this aspect of cultural sociology, which will also include the definition of its (critical) positions in relation to Marxism, English Cultural Studies, and the sociology of Pierre Bourdieu.

3

A Critique of Marx, Cultural Studies, and Bourdieu

Alexander's reading of Marx contains several key elements for his own theoretical and analytical project. First, it is significant because Parsons had deliberately ignored Marx in the synthesis offered in *The Structure of Social Action* (and its sequels, such as *The Social System*), so Alexander's critique thus reflects a more comprehensive synthesis of the sociological tradition. Secondly, this reading is important because it allows Alexander to position himself critically in relation to the materialist reductionism promoted by Marx (and by Marxism in its aftermath), giving a more significant place to culture (and religion, as we have seen with Durkheim, and with Weber in the next chapter).[1] Finally, on a more properly epistemological level, this critique also shows the definition Alexander gives to critique, which enables him to elaborate a "critique of the critique" that clearly demonstrates a properly reflexive sociology. This last point seems to me particularly important, not only because it orients Alexander's later critique of English Cultural Studies and Bourdieu's sociology (together with that of the Frankfurt School), but also because it touches the core theoretical project of cultural sociology in relation to the main contemporary developments of the discipline.

Let us simply say that "criticism" has undergone many rearrangements since its official entry into modern Western philosophy with Immanuel Kant, and in its aftermath with Hegel and Marx. It is useful to recall here that Kant's three Critiques had been established against dogmatism (essentially theology), but only according to their limited capacities: for Kant, "critical" philosophy succeeded only in delimiting the conditions of possibility according to which human knowledge could express its rights, leaving a place outside of itself for divine knowledge (and its reflection in theology).[2] Consequentially, from the point of view of the theoretical knowledge of nature expressed in the *Critique of Pure Reason*, experience must agree with an already given natural framework (which it is possible to know by filling in pre-existing conceptual forms, accessed by intuition and schematism through sense experience) because it is created and known in its ultimate depths (if not its intention) by divinity alone. This position will be continued in modern science, which recognizes the objectivity of knowledge in its capacity to associate objects of experience with a pre-existing nature – without admitting, as contemporary science does, its own presence and activity as a condition of access not only to this knowledge of objects but also to their creation. This edifice of critical philosophy is going to topple entirely with the Hegelian critique, which places the *science of logic* as the only base of the unity of the knowledge of nature and (human) spirit.[3] The "critical" moment will thus be absorbed in the movement of a dialectical logic, leaving nothing outside itself; this is the definition that Hegel gives to the "Absolute," which makes it correspond to the very content of the "divine" such as it is then expressed in its human forms – that is to say, in the respective figures of art, religion, and science. In his criticism of Hegel, Marx will situate the dialectic at the very heart of nature (and of the human being in history), and his own "criticism" of society will then paradoxically situate knowledge in an "exterior" to present society. This opens onto the utopia of its revolutionary transformation, which comes back in a certain way to the Kantian position in response to dogmatism, recognized by Marx not only in religion but in any form of ideology, and even in culture, including that of modern bourgeois society itself with its political institutions. We can thus see that Alexander chooses, at least implicitly, the

Hegelian way of situating logic (and the immanent critical moment that belongs to it). However, the inherent dialectical character is not always explicitly situated, which at times makes his position relatively ambiguous (which is apparent, among other things, in his attachment to religion and to the religious within society).[4] In this way, though, he will put himself in a position to criticize Marx's sociology, particularly his criticism of the capitalist bourgeois society which motivates towards its "final destination." This "critique of the critique" represents the theoretical logic of Alexander's project, cultural sociology, which sees in Marxism, beyond its materialist reductionism, the impossibility of reflexivity (Alexander 1982b: 62).

The rejection of Marxian critique

I say "final destination" because Alexander, like many contemporary critics, sees in Marx's early writings elements that could have oriented his sociology in quite a different way. When Marx, in his critique of Hegelian philosophy and desire to go beyond the materialist positions of Feuerbach, approaches questions of (subjective) alienation and the material conditions of production of existence, there is the possibility of connecting to a coherent vision of a human life where individual existence is situated in its fundamental sociality, without this being excessively problematic. With the introduction, however, of political economy – the relation between exploitation and the exclusion produced by private property (and the subordination of labor to capital that this implies) – and the scheme of historical development covering all the development of humanity after "primitive communism," Marx resolutely commits himself, according to Alexander, to an instrumental definition of action. He also commits himself to a definition of the social order under capitalism (until its eventual overthrow in the revolution), from which paradoxically emerges the "messianic" character of this analysis, tied to the "laws of history" deduced from a reading of the revolutions that marked the development of humanity, as outlined clearly in the *Communist Manifesto* of 1848. There does remain an "exterior" to this critique, but it is situated in the utopian horizon of the proletarian revolution, which renders the critique de facto inoperative from the point of view of its own reflexivity, since, as Alexander asks: where can this philosophical expression of the critique come from, if not from the very society whose contradictions it reflects, being itself an expression of a "superstructure" inevitably in touch with its "base"? (Alexander 1982b: 203–5.) Here, it is the "residual categories" of Marxian analysis (such as "false consciousness" and "class consciousness") that come to play a much more important role in the revolutionary process than Marx himself is willing to admit. Moreover, how can such a sociology renounce human history as it has been lived (by criticizing religion or any other form of "ideological" (mis)representation) while claiming to be external to these developments? Marx's answer to these questions, the particular or exceptional character of criticism, coupled with the reliance on a "dialectical materialism" associated with positive science, cannot satisfy the theoretical logic of sociology. Alexander thus points directly to the heart of Marxian logic by showing how the confusion between the instrumental action defined by political economy and the definition of human production becomes, through the reification of the commodity and the institutional "superstructure" of private property and politics, a way of confining any objective definition of the social order to a discussion only of a capitalist order that imposes itself on all individuals. This renders criticism inoperative, except when it resorts to "external" imperatives that it cannot account for analytically, such as the communist utopia, the autonomy of individual consciousness, and the science of dialectical materialism itself (ibid.: 187–210). Marx's legacy, through a series of rereadings and interpretations (from Kautsky to Lenin and Trostky, from Lukács to Gramsci, from Sartre to Lefebvre and Althusser, and from Marcuse to Habermas, etc.), will only lead Alexander back to the dead ends of a critique of political economy incapable of really getting rid of its fundamental principles. Marxian thought generally reduces action to its instrumental character and confuses the normative order with the strict and narrow aims of capitalism erected as a dogma that cannot be surpassed (except in utopia). It is in this spirit, as a "critique of the critique," that English Cultural Studies and the sociology of Bourdieu will be approached.

Critique of Cultural Studies

Alexander explicitly rejects the neo-Marxist theory developed in England, which served as the foundation for Cultural Studies (Sherwood et al. 1993). This position is important from at least two points of view: first, it comes in the context of clarifying a possible orientation of "cultural sociology," which is still waiting for the formulation of its "strong program" – let us recall that the subtitle of the Durkheim-inspired book published by Alexander in 1988 explicitly links it to Cultural Studies (as does the important article he co-authored with Philip Smith in 1993, "The Discourse of American Civil Society: A New Proposal for Cultural Studies"). Secondly, Cultural Studies, seen in the perspective of a competition against other analytical possibilities, particularly that of the nascent cultural sociology, will serve to firm up the definition of culture which the rest of Alexander's sociological project will deal with.[5] But this opposition must also be perceived in relation to Cultural Studies' engagement with questions associated with *power* (political as well as cultural), plus the inscription within the framework of an analysis of social dynamics that furnish civil society. This has implications that are as much disciplinary (i.e. with regard to the different analytical stakes and levels of consideration, whether epistemological, theoretical, or empirical, that they imply) as, let us say, "national," for cultural sociology's reply to Cultural Studies easily takes a polemical (if not political) turn by foregrounding the different contexts at work on either side of the Atlantic.

The tradition of Cultural Studies has its origins in the Centre for Contemporary Culture Studies (CCCS) established at the University of Birmingham in the early 1970s, based on the work of Richard Hoggart and Raymond Williams in the 1950s and 1960s. This work, initially carried out within the framework of courses offered to working-class adults, aimed to encourage the development of a cultural vision dissociated from the vision of dominant culture within English society.

The initial aim was to show that culture could be understood from a "popular" perspective, mostly opposed to the aspirations of bourgeois culture (as well as the residual aristocratic culture within English society). The "emerging" culture represented this rise of the working classes, which was targeted by the studies of culture presented by certain intellectuals associated with the movement of the "New Left" (grouped in part around the *New Left Review*), strongly inspired by Marxism and closely associated with the British Labour Party.[6] With the arrival of Stuart Hall on the scene, Cultural Studies blossomed by proposing the introduction of a strong semiotic perspective, anchored in the dual capacity of "codification"/"decodification," which intervenes on the level of social meanings. Thus, for Hall, the symbols associated with the dominant culture can very well be contested or subverted in their reception by the popular classes, a "decodification" that they can then operate to their advantage.[7] All that previously passed for a reification and a consequent alienation reigning within the framework of mass culture (as had been characterized by the Frankfurt School, in the criticism led by Adorno and Horkheimer in the immediate post-war period, for example) thus found a new analytical version, ready to grant social actors an autonomy in the contestation of symbolic forms being imposed by the dominant culture. The development of Cultural Studies, an analytical current that became very important in Britain and in the English-speaking world in the 1970s and 1980s, had also spread to the United States, and it was this spread, this "British imperialism" expressed on the analytical level, that Alexander and his colleagues were to argue against.[8] And this was in the sociopolitical context of the collapse of communist regimes (in the post-Berlin wall era), and not of capitalist democracies, as the authors point out. This aspect of things will be particularly reflected in Alexander's theorization of the "civil sphere," as we will see in the following chapters.

Alexander's critique of Cultural Studies thus retains much of his earlier criticism of Marx and Marxism, but it also accentuates it by raising the issue of a definition of culture that is not simply engaged in power struggles. This critique highlights five principles that are the basis of Cultural Studies' analytic frame:

1 that institutional structures are hierarchical and oppressive, without recognizing that the social order is also voluntaristic and intersubjective in character;
2 that culture is not only linked to power but is actually reduced to it, highlighting the importance of the concept of *articulation* of power relations;
3 that it is mainly the concepts of hegemony and counter-hegemony that govern cultural forms, which are always perceived as the locus of struggle;
4 that action is "informed" by culture and thus always strategic in character and bound to the struggles of daily life; and
5 that the theoretical enterprise has to be profoundly ideological and act in favor of dominated, repressed, and marginalized populations (Sherwood et al. 1993: 371).

Alexander and his colleagues point out that social actors possess sufficient reflexivity to "participate in the codes and narratives of a culture that encircles power and reflects upon it." By emphasizing the subjectivity of actors and their perceptions, one can also go beyond a strictly "material" understanding of society in terms of meanings and bring out more creative, synthetic, and objective socio-structural approaches that account for social meanings, not simply resorting to a meta-narrative of oppression and emancipation. They argue for the recognition of an analytical current opposed to Cultural Studies. For them, there is no point in considering that analysis serves to "demystify" culture; on the contrary, it is necessary to show how actors manage to "re-mystify" their social worlds: "despite the continuous disappointments and degradations of the modern world, persons manage to maintain their beliefs in transcendental values and 'true' solidarity, how they still fear evil and persevere in their pursuit of the good, and how they engage in ritual renewal rather than strategic behavior" (Sherwood et al. 1993: 372, 375). This criticism, which will also be leveled at Bourdieu's analytical approach (as well as certain aspects of Weber's thought), highlights the orientation of cultural sociology with a full confirmation of its fundamental principles. And although it leaves the question of power in temporary abeyance, it also draws attention to analytical axes that will become the definitive landmarks of its theoretical advances.[9]

Critique of Bourdieusian determinism

Alexander's critique of Bourdieu continues this critique of Cultural Studies, as Bourdieu is placed directly in the wake of the "neo-Marxist" orientation that appeared in the 1960s.[10] As with Cultural Studies, we can understand that part of the importance of this critique is the growing influence of Bourdieu in the United States since the mid-1980s, largely due to the presence of influential former students of Bourdieu, such as Loïc Wacquant and Michèle Lamont, which constituted an obstacle in the development of cultural sociology.[11] But there is another aspect of Bourdieu's sociology that is perhaps the most decisive element in Alexander's critique of him: Bourdieu explicitly defines his approach, as early as the 1960s, as an open critique of structuralism, relying in part on the pragmatist tradition to "recover the actor and the meaningfulness of her world" (Alexander 1995: 130). As Alexander himself claims to be a member of both traditions of thought (employing them in a completely different, even antithetical, way), it is clear that the confrontation with Bourdieu constitutes a decisive step in order to differentiate himself from the latter from an analytical point of view, and at the same time wanting to contest the positivistic scientific character claimed by the Bourdieusian approach through its presumed complexity and richness.

It is not a question for Alexander of denying the originality of Bourdieu's theoretical "inventions"; rather, it is a matter of attacking the presuppositions that they mask, deconstructing them to reveal their flaws. These come from two fundamental criticisms addressed to Bourdieu which take up the principles of theoretical logic advanced by Alexander. On the one hand, the concepts elaborated by Bourdieu (mainly those of *habitus* and "fields") entail a reduction of analytical possibilities with regard to the understanding of social life; on the other, these concepts, as well as the analyses they allow, are irremediably tainted with the fundamental determinism that reduces action to its utilitarian and strategic character while assuming the irreversible persistence of the capitalist system. These two defects mean that Bourdieu cannot escape the constricted view characteristic of Marx and his epigones, despite attempting to critique Marxism by reorienting it towards an understanding of culture in its autonomous, symbolic forms. This motivated Bourdieu in the 1960s and 1970s, inspired by the ethnographic analytical work he conducted in Algeria (Alexander 1995: 130–1). While linked to the French intellectual context that saw the emergence of important figures (Althusser, Lévi-Strauss, Foucault, etc.), Bourdieu also distanced himself from them. On the one hand, he tried to avoid easy reifications and outrageous simplifications in his criticisms of structuralism (Lévi-Strauss in particular), though he overlooked the flexibility offered by "bricolage" in the reformulation of myths by actors. On the other hand, while claiming to escape symbolic determinations affecting behavior, he reinscribed them even more deeply in the "unconscious" of actors, who then merely reproduce the structures in which they are engaged (ibid.: 132–4). The concept of *habitus* is the best example of these character- istics, since it acts through subjectivities as a mechanism that inexorably traps them in an unconscious transmission of social practices and positions – annihilating any possibility of subjective reflexivity – although Bourdieu was appar- ently inspired here by the interactionist currents associated with American pragmatism. According to Alexander, despite Bourdieu's efforts to show that the "structured–structuring" character of *habitus* allows transformations on the level of social practices, all his analyses in fact confirm the rigidity of this concept, which inescapably reproduces the social order that puts it in play. This social order, itself hierarchical in character and fundamentally centered on domination, appears in a static form associated with the practically immutable structures of social relations. The worst example of this static reproduction is found in Bourdieu's concept of the "field," based on Weber, which attempts to precisely show the diversity of areas of organized practices within the social order. Although fields suggest a "relative autonomy" in their capacity to structure symbolic relations according to diverse interests (in the domains of education, sport, art, consumption, etc.), they are actually all brought back to the level of the social order (ibid.: 183–6). This is reflected in Bourdieu's other foundational concepts such as "cultural capital" and "symbolic power," which in fact only serve to translate the imperatives of a normative order based on utilitarian action and the unlimited competition of individuals and social classes. It is thus through a "general economy," or rather through a reproduction of the principles of utilitarian economy in all spheres of social life, that the Bourdieusian analysis is realized (ibid.: 157). This conception depends on the principle of "structural homologies," which establishes automatic correspondences between the social order founded on the utilitarian economic norm, all the "fields" that fall automatically under its implicit jurisdiction, and all the registers of *habitus* that unconsciously determine the actions of all individual subjectivities (ibid.: 161–4).[12] However, this logic succeeds only with great difficulty in justifying analytical reflexivity itself, especially in a "critical" capacity and in an eminently paradoxical way: this analytical reflexivity is completely compromised in its role of revealing the perennial structures of domination, while using the cover of "objectivity" to clear itself of participating in these very structures (ibid.: 192).

The shortcomings identified by Alexander in Bourdieu's theoretical and analytical work are largely linked to his understanding of "interests," which structure the fields in different symbolic ways and motivate subjectivities in their actions. But because of the reduction of which these are again the object, and of their practically universal determinism, these "interests" are finally linked to the sole *egoistic* pursuit of privileged positions in any field and of the advantages that individuals can accumulate in the course of their social existence. This culminates in the position that even altruism is in fact a disguised egoism, a way of acting in one's own interest – this would ultimately become Bourdieu's "political ontology."[13] Here, even so-called anthropological positions, such as that of Mauss's system of gifts and counter-gifts, are in fact reduced to nothing, ruining all the efforts of such thinkers (not only Mauss, but also Freud and Elias) to grasp the fundamental motive of any civilization when it comes to the sublimation of relations that allow peaceful cohabitation within a consensual social order, above all deferred in its purposes, as some other critics have pointed out. Privileging in this way the determinism of the struggle of all against all "makes it impossible for Bourdieu to understand democracy itself" (Alexander 1995: 152).[14]

This last criticism appears to be conclusive, and it also prepares the ground for what cultural sociology perhaps envisages as its ultimate task: to come to grips with the democratic spirit that could be at the heart of our societies, and which manifests itself through a capacity for symbolic expression reflexively linked to the very structures of contemporary mass democracies reflected in the "civil sphere." It is in relation to this issue that one understands Alexander's remarks at the end of his critique of Bourdieu, where he underlines the impossibility for Bourdieusian analysis to pose the question of public sphere as a site of political/institutional reflexivity. In this way he contrasts Bourdieusian cynicism with the utopianism of Habermas, who aimed to theorize bourgeois public sphere in a society that has resolutely gone beyond the categories of modern society. Alexander pleads for such a category, which he would later call the *civil sphere*. It remains to be shown just how the question of political power – implicated in an almost equally important way in Marxism, Cultural Studies, and Bourdieu's sociology – can then be restated according to new parameters. These are given in principle in the post-positivist approach already described, and it is according to the theoretical logic that strives to elaborate a multidimensional approach that they will have to be accomplished; in other words, analysis produced in this way expresses reflexively as a "critique of the critique," attempting to go beyond the limitations of the only "critique" of Marxian origin.

Critical theory and reflexivity: the power of representation

As we can see, Alexander's "critique of the critique" – from Marx to Bourdieu, including Marxism of all kinds and Cultural Studies – will prepare the ground for the expression of a new theoretical and analytical position; the project of cultural sociology will be articulated around a political reflection, using the principles of a religious sociology to frame how social practices are structured within contemporary societies. In this reorientation of Cultural Studies, the reflexive capacity of the actors becomes central, as well as the capacity of analysis and theory to exhibit this reflexivity. The emphasis of cultural sociology thus lands on civil society, on knowing how to be at one with the evolution of contemporary society in a way that is not "critical" but, rather, by means of the "critique of the critique," reflexively engaged in active participation with the social world (Alexander and Smith 1993). Before that, however, some obstacles must be removed, not the least of which is to rethink modernity and its aftermath to re-evaluate the diagnoses that classical sociology (primarily Weber) has provided. It is indeed by turning to Weber that Alexander conceives that one can, and indeed must, return to the question of Reason within modernity, not only as a central motive of its development but especially because of the economicist, technical, and ultimately reductive force of "rationalization" in the context of modern society. Against the "disenchantment of the world" described by Weber, Alexander will try to reverse the sociological project of a sociology of religion by showing its extensions in the contemporary world in order to revive a certain enthusiasm for political practices.

This also means that Alexander's position will make political representation play a role that it could no longer assume from a critical view of modern bourgeois society. Since Marx, and in Marxism in general, as well as critical theory, Cultural Studies, and Bourdieusian sociology, the critique of bourgeois institutions was aimed at denouncing the alienation, reification, and domination associated with the capitalist mode of production, so the critique of this critique will have to take an entirely different turn with respect to these questions. The effect of the Marxian critique, which began in the early 1840s in the manuscript *Critique of Political Philosophy* (1843) attacking Hegel's philosophy, and which continued throughout the critical tradition, was paradoxically to politicize all social relations (beginning, of course, with those circumscribed by the capitalist economy in the opposition between labor and capital) at the same time as it discredited the sphere of political representation in modern bourgeois society. Political *representation*, a distorted ideological reflection of class relations governed by economic domination, thus fell directly into the abyss of superstructures incapable of corresponding to the real social struggles taking place in society. The critical tradition claims that all aspects of a society based on a capitalist political economy (from consumption to education) could only reproduce the struggles taking place under the guise of disalienation, anti-domination, and emancipation. The critique of the critique that Alexander proposes turns this position on its head by bringing back to the political, and especially to political representation, the essential agonistic struggles linked to power. This analysis involves studies of performance and social theatricality, using the analysis of social movements inspired by Touraine and others. The representation of power, in all its virtualities linked to the contemporary political world, will thus be shown through the power of representation.

This way of considering contemporary political life assigns a new task to criticism. It has to respond to the diffusion of political power in society, which the Marxian critique had envisaged in a practical way, so to speak, by implicitly and explicitly politicizing all aspects of social life through its critique of modern bourgeois political institutions, but also by simultaneously bypassing their relations to these institutions. This diffusion of power is easily seen, for example, when one considers the generalization of citizenship in the transition from modern bourgeois democracies to postmodern mass democracies. It is, however, within the context of the latter that Alexander will attempt to reconsider political diffusion by concentrating on the representations of power – of the dominant class, as analyzed for example in his studies on Obama's presidency (Alexander and Jaworski 2014; Alexander 2011a, 2010a), as much as the power of the dominated, in studies on social and cultural trauma (Alexander 2012a; Eyerman et al. 2011; Alexander et al. 2004). Critique is thus situated here in the evaluation of political representation of all kinds and has been required to show their respective limits. It is only with this perspective that it manages in fact to demonstrate, in a dialectical way, the limited effect of the *representation of power* through the mechanisms of the *power of representation*.

Within this framework Alexander will theorize what he calls the "civil sphere" in which to deploy his analyses; however, in doing so, he confronts the theoretical renewal proposed by Jürgen Habermas in his theory of "communicative action," located downstream of his well-known work *The Structural Transformation of the Public Sphere* (1962). Alexander's interest in Habermas began in the mid-1980s, and he developed it in a way that would deeply affect his own work, as a competing theorization to the proposal by the representative of the Frankfurt School.[15] In his long and thorough review of the first volume of Habermas's *The Theory of Communicative Action* (*Reason and the Rationalization of Society*), Alexander (1985b) first notes that the Habermasian turn in critical theory definitively moves it away from the revolutionary project inherited from Marxism. Relying, among other things, on a reading of Weber that Alexander considers original, Habermas managed to reconstruct the sociological tradition beyond Marxism, even offering an extraordinary perspective on "what Weber's cultural sociology of modernity might have been" by broadening its "conception of rationality" (ibid.: 407, 409). Habermas effected this enrichment of the sociological perspective by bringing in, on the one hand, the psychology of Piaget and, on the other, the legal forms of contemporary societies, based on a "post-conventional" rationality largely derived from bourgeois democracies that emphasized individual autonomy and contractual obligations. The challenge for Habermas was thus to define a "communicational rationality" as the basis for a new way of posing the question of reason, freed from its strictly "transcendental" nature and oriented more directly towards the world of life or experience. If rational action in Weberian sociology was held in the narrow frame of *Zweckrationalität* – action strictly defined in the relationship of means to an end in a technical or instrumental-utilitarian sense largely endorsed by the capitalist system – it is instead for Habermas a question of opening this action to its communicative virtualities by counting on intersubjective agreement (and even on an agreement established "without constraint"). Action perceived according to this perspective is thus no longer "instrumental" but, rather, "communicative." Habermas derived the possibilities of communicative activity from Austin's philosophy of language – discarding its only "strategic" orientation in power relations, but not counting on the *performative* dimension either (as Alexander will do) – but this was insufficient to consolidate his model on anything but a so-called utopian basis. Alexander also points out that Habermas's reading of Parsons in the second volume of *The Theory of Communicative Action – Lifeworld and Systems, a Critique of Functionalist Reason* – situates his enterprise as a consideration of the most promising advances in sociological theory from the point of view of its systematicity. Habermas would even play with a possible opposition between "systems" and "lifeworld," where the latter does not in fact rest on any solid conception of what *culture* could be when envisaged through a sociology that truly relies on the symbolic modalities expressed by Durkheim, among others. In short, while holding Habermas's effort to be a substantial achievement, Alexander considers that it fails to lay the groundwork for a consistent analysis of contemporary society, and that his renewal of Marxism and critical theory does not produce a valid analytical model in this context. When he comes to reflect retrospectively on this reading of Habermas, Alexander will point out that it was from this moment that the possibility emerged to orient his own enterprise in a much more pronounced way towards an integration of semiotics, poststructuralism, and hermeneutics, and to couple them with his desire to redefine convincing analytical paths for his own sociological project (Alexander 2005a).

Alexander's distance from critical theory developed beyond Habermas's work, consolidated by the way he positioned himself towards the work of Axel Honneth, who proposed another version of the critical tradition of the Frankfurt School through the problematic of recognition, beginning in the 1990s. Honneth's thought is based on a return to the Hegelian struggle of individuals for their mutual self-recognition (reconciled in the terms of the interactionist pragmatism of George Herbert Mead), reflection on social traumas, the "society of disrespect" that generates them, and ways of envisaging a new normativity within contemporary society. These themes will be taken up, in parallel so to speak, and without particular or systematic attention to Honneth's work, by cultural sociology, culminating in the theorization of the civil sphere, social and cultural traumas, and the performativity of social movements and symbolic expressions carried by specific actors and groups in the contemporary socio-political dynamic. The same could be said, with the required nuance of course, about the work of the French theorists Thévenot and Boltanski, who, following the initial inspiration of Bourdieu, pursued the development of a critical theory that has parallels with the work of their German colleagues, by integrating certain aspects of pragmatism. We will deal with these questions in chapters 5 and 6, but, before doing so, we must focus on the way in which Alexander rereads Weber's sociology, which will allow him to develop all the material necessary for the consolidation of a sociology fundamentally centered on culture. It is indeed by delving into the study of Weber's sociology of culture, and particularly his sociology of religion, that Alexander will succeed in his own developing a "cultural sociology," where even the question of reason and its fate within (post)modernity will be engaged to overcome the aporias of the Frankfurt theorists – and of Weber himself.

4

Culture, Politics, and Civil Religion: Weber and Beyond

Max Weber is of specific interest to Alexander in at least three ways: first, Weber's sociology of religion takes over from Durkheim's by examining the great monotheistic religions of history – whereas Durkheim had only analyzed totemism as the basic model of all religions. Second, Weber's sociology, as presented in his great work *Economy and Society*, proposes a synthesis of religion and economy and managed to overcome the antinomies of idealism and materialism previously identified in Durkheim and Marx, thus opening up a "multidimensional" study of social life. And, third, by tackling the problem of rationality as the central figure of *historical individuality* that constitutes Western society (though without excluding the "irrational" counterpart of the spiritual), Weber posed in an innovative – but no less problematic – way the challenge of deciding on the destiny of this central modern category within contemporary society. These three complementary planes are crucial for the development of cultural sociology, for they constitute – in addition to the lessons drawn from Durkheim, Marx, and Parsons – the backdrop against which all of Alexander's original analyses will be oriented. Paradoxically, however, because of their emblematic character they become the object of Alexander's threefold critique of Weber and thus take on this singular prominence. First, Alexander considers that Weber's sociology of religion errs in the proposed analysis of the last of the great religions of history resulting from the schism of Christianity – that is to say, Protestantism (and in particular its Puritan strain) – by showing how this ends up in a secularization of the world that manages to exhaust the meaning of all religious commitments. Second, he proposes the idea that Weber, while succeeding in multidimensionally establishing the relations between individual action and the normative social order on the historical level, reduces the complexity of these relations to the one-dimensional character of instrumental or technical action (*Zweckrationalität*) within the framework of contemporary society, thus rendering ineffective the historical sociological program that he had so brilliantly elaborated. Finally, as a consequence of the first two criticisms, Alexander posits that Weber's pessimistic diagnosis of the fate of reason in modern Western society is simply wrong, since it succeeds, beyond the "disenchantment" it portrays, only in illustrating the emotional dryness and intellectual emptiness of a world definitively locked into Weber's metaphor of the "iron cage."

Alexander's interpretation of Weber's sociology places it clearly above those of Durkheim and Marx, for the simple reason that he sees in it a synthesis of the antinomies produced between idealism and materialism, which respectively tainted these two pioneering enterprises (Alexander 1983a). While the volume he devotes to the critical reading of Weberian sociology is similar to the previous volume on Durkheim and Marx in that it focuses on the early writings and then on the late writings, it cannot draw the same interpretative follow-ups, due in particular to the biographical hazards that affected Weber (his nervous breakdown during the years 1897–1902 and his premature death in 1920, at the age of fifty-six).[1] Nevertheless, Alexander insists on a discontinuity between the 1889–97 writings of the economic historian and the more resolutely sociological writings after 1902 within the specific ideological context of Bismarckian Germany. During this time, debates between social democrats and socialists raged alongside intellectual and methodological quarrels within the then emerging human sciences, culminating pessimistically in the immediate aftermath of World War I. All the richness of Weber's analyses comes from this bubbling German context, where the writings of Marx and Marxism were fighting against approaches that advocated a sociology of culture within the university academy,[2] and where the question of historical evolution (of Germany and the world) was debated in relation to the political stakes of the time. Rather than reading the materialism of political economy and the idealism of religious representations back to back, Weber tries to show their reciprocal implications through an interpretation attentive to the possibilities of their multidimensional, interwoven relationships. According to the different contexts of historical development, individual action is then significantly oriented by a normative order that varies according to the contingencies that intervene as practical and ideal determinants, at times favoring either the maintenance of slavery in antiquity or the emergence of a bourgeois class during the modern era. This reflects not so much a form of transhistorical determinism, so to speak, as an attempt to understand the detours through which meanings with a specific "origin" and "end" (not so much a "telos" as a "finite" character, limited in time and space) are formed in history.[3] This capacity of Weberian analysis to shift attention from one aspect of historical development to another leads to the multidimensional capacity of representation that Alexander thematizes in a very positive way. At times, this shift supports specific determinations that give substance to a given context, either in terms of individual meanings that emerge from the point of view of the actors or in terms of the openings or closures of the whole social order in the face of these meanings. Alexander celebrates this in spite of the fact that it is explicitly posed as a way of precisely defining the historical relativity of any meaning, which will become a feature of cultural sociology, concerned for its part to show the persistence of perennial meanings by associating them to a cultural tradition (or to a "civil religion"). Alexander supports his criticism on this side of a theoretical logic not entirely achieved in Weber's early writings, but reversed in the eventual diagnosis that he will make of modernity.

In his historical sociology, as much as in his sociology of religion or law, Weber posits this multidimensional analytical capacity as an idealistic formalization of forms of motivation for action. The well-known fourfold division between emotional (or affectual), traditional, value (*Wertrationalität*) and instrumental (*Zweckrationalität*) meaning testifies to an analytical enterprise capable of attending to precise socio-historical contexts by focusing on one or several of these characteristics of individual activity in relation to a specific social order that varies over time. Weber thus shows an analytical flexibility that takes into account both the ideal possibilities and the material means of concretizing them, without relying on a radical dichotomy between them. As Alexander points out, this analytic multidimensionality reveals a synthetic perspective that is not only innovative but also extremely fertile for comprehensively understanding meanings in a situation – as Weber posits in his properly sociological definition of action. Alexander, however, is not paying attention to the fact that the Weberian "ideal-typical" characterization introduces a certain rigidity in what can be considered as the dialectic, and therefore plasticity, inherent in symbolic forms.[4] Alexander does not then directly criticize this, as he will himself eventually use the "ideal-type" method, but he will end up challenging the terms of Weber's sociological analysis because of its reduction in the under-standing of action and order within contemporary society (Alexander 1983a: 22–9).

However, Weber does not attempt this reduction of meaning in his sociology of religion, since he manages, on the contrary, to show how the great monotheistic religions of the world in fact unified the ideal and material dimensions of individual action and the social order. Alexander therefore fully supports those analyses in which Weber shows a flexible and truly multidimensional analytical understanding. Here, Weber avoids both Durkheim's idealist orientation, which detached religious representations to a certain extent from material requirements and contingencies (if not from the "instrumental rationality" present in certain forms of religion, such as Confucianism and Puritanism), and the materialist orientation of Marx, who systematically lowered the representations of the social order to the level of material class interests, reducing any religious form to its opioid effects (ibid.: 39–50). But it is not only the sociology of religion (and the sociology of law) in which Weber shows this analytical prodigality. Alexander notes that, in Weber's study of the city, his analysis operates with the same intelligence and insight in its ability to grasp the different characters of the urban phenomenon in relation to the various meanings deployed according to different historical contexts – especially the quite particular character of the city as produced by "conjuration" in the bourgeois communes. All the ingredients of a sociology based on a broad definition of culture are indeed combined here, including religion, law, and the economy, as well as a unified vision of the social order shared among individuals, emphasizing the general sense of an "urban revolution" as the typical form of political association in the development of European modernity (ibid.: 53–5). This is obviously important in Alexander's eyes, on the one hand, to show the validity of Weberian analytics in what it discovers as the specific character of bourgeois modernity within European society and, on the other, because it constitutes a kind of model that can be updated for cultural sociology – and will be asserted in Alexander's theorization of the civil sphere. However, because of the unfulfilled promises of Weber in his analysis of modernity, Alexander will want to critically return to its ultimate expressions, particularly when it is a question of deploying the original meanings retained by cultural sociology – as he had done for Durkheim's *The Elementary Forms of Religious Life* – but according to different elements of theorization.

With Weber and beyond: a sociology of religion in modernity

Weber introduced a decisive inflection in his analytical path when he published *The Protestant Ethic and the Spirit of Capitalism*. In this work, as we know, the articulation between the Protestant religious orientation and the meaning of instrumental practices takes a turn that is both definitive and, so to speak, dramatic – if not downright tragic – resulting in an irremediable dichotomy between the two and the confinement of action to a normative order definitively cut off from its spiritual significance (and/ or from its other "rational in value," "traditional," and "affectual" components). The "iron cage" from which the spirit flew (voluntarily chosen in the Protestant religious framework by a strict morality codifying behavior in view of spiritual salvation) gradually and finally imposed itself as the iron law of capitalism oriented by instrumental action, guided in a solely mechanical way by the logical imperatives of a "technical rationality" that unfolds throughout the entire horizon of contemporary society – but presumably without soul and spirit. Weber's pessimism about the fate of modernity is matched only by the implacable and inescapable analytical verdict he renders. Alexander takes note of this verdict, but shows that it contradicts the principles of a truly multidimensional analysis by making "instrumental action" the only meaning given both to individual practices and the social order within contemporary society. This reduction is abusive, according to Alexander, though Weber himself would not have perceived that his own analyses were in fact open to other perspectives. This is what Alexander intends to show, not only from the point of view of the sociology of religion but also in the fields of law and politics, where Weber also reduced meaning to its narrow utilitarian function. He did this in law by reducing the rationality inherent in the social order to its mainly economic (this is undoubtedly where Weber comes closest to Marx) and bureaucratic ends; he did this in politics by reducing it to the organization of "parties," which always play the game of sectarian interests by adhering to rational aims defined through "instrumental action," which only privileges strategic views aligned with the acquisition of power.

These determinations converge towards a one-sided analysis of modernity. It is the analysis of Protestantism, and in particular its so-called extreme form Puritanism, that serves as Weber's fulcrum for sealing the fate of modernity. Yet, as Alexander points out, Weber's few analyses of his brief experience in the United States, in the four-month trip he made there in 1904 with his wife Marianne, already show significant deviations from the religious practices he observed there from their European counterparts. Returning to Weber's short 1906 text "Churches and Sects in North America," Alexander proposes a bold interpretation: he sees in it nothing less than an observation of the cleavage that exists between the meaning religious modernization has taken in the United States and that which it possesses in Europe, particularly in Germany.[5] This cleavage has more significance than initially appears to be the case, since it reveals a completely different orientation of Protestant religious activity within American society. Weber had indeed noted the "worldly" character that religious affiliation acquired in the United States, emphasizing that participation in the cult activities of a Protestant sect was in fact equivalent not so much to the inner spiritual significance of individuals as to the social probity that it granted them – especially in the field of economic affairs.[6] The inflection towards social recognition definitely takes precedence, in this context, over ecclesiastical obedience, even if the latter is relative to the sect, and it remains decisive in the Protestant context, where sectarianism multiplies the possibilities of theological dispute. In other words, as Weber forcefully underlines, it is the "social grouping" that appears to be the predominant marker of individual social identity, in the form of sects or other forms of organization (Weber 2003). This reversal in the interpretation of the social value of grouping, which explicitly returns to a dialectical inversion of Ferdinand Tönnies's opposition between *Gemeinschaft* and *Gesellschaft*, rather produces a *religious* connotation to the activity of "social grouping" by showing the modern and practically contractual character of collective religious organization.[7] In the political framework of mass democracy in the United States, where the rule of law must prevail over religious associations (since the constitution guarantees freedom of worship), the cult grouping thus maintains, according to Alexander, a "fierce commitment and an almost fanatical concern for substantive obedience to the spirit of the law," where "the passion that sects demand in the religious life of the laity, fosters principled and radical forms of political participation" (Alexander 1989: 108). We can thus see how, in the North American context, the Protestant religious orientation takes on a properly political value of active participation in social life, because it enjoins the individual to consider his activity or action in the sense of belonging to a "grouping," which in turn acquires a politico-religious value. Alexander will therefore consider this reversal as having a much wider overall meaning, likely not only to counter the Weberian pessimism about the fate of modernity but also to relaunch it on bases that are entirely reopened to a truly contrary meaning. For Alexander, this is a resolutely "optimistic" reading of the American political experience, which thus discovers a different morality within its own modernity, constituted by "civil religion."

Weberian analytics is then criticized according to the reductions it has called for in its interpretation of modernity. Activity reduced to "instrumental action" does not become the only way of development, but it must deal with the other dimensions that Weber had relegated to the oblivion of history. Thus, charisma, coming from strong personalities and capable of founding social orders, and its subsequent routinization in bureaucratized forms – religious or juridical – appears central within an analysis sensitive to the performances of political actors, while the domination of the "iron cage" finds determinations capable of orientations other than those of disenchantment with respect to history and the destiny of modernity (Alexander 1983a: 81–96).[8] One should not interpret Alexander drawing from these criticisms of Weberian sociology a simple unilaterally positive, "re-enchanting" analysis of modernity; rather, his global diagnosis, such as he will express in *The Dark Side of Modernity* (Alexander 2013a), will aim at showing the two sides of this historical development and its consequences. But we must remember that, for Alexander, in a way that becomes clearer in comparison with Durkheim and Weber, "[s]ocial theory is an attempt to address the problem of meaning in a de-divinized world." Beyond its capacity to offer "mechanical explanations of the facts," it must succeed in establishing "their meaning in a more generalized and existential sense" and provide "a kind of self-reflection unavailable in traditional life, a 'rational' way to approach metaphysical issues that even the most modern man or woman still desperately needs" (Alexander 1989: 69). It is on the basis of this principle that cultural sociology can take much further the multidimensional analysis detected in Weber, but also by drawing on other sources can such an undertaking eventually lead to convincing results, both on the theoretical level and in terms of empirical analyses, in accordance with the principles of the "strong program."

Weberian analysis reassessed by pragmatics and hermeneutics

Weber's historical sociology can serve as a point of reference for the rest of Alexander's analytical program because it opens up, almost naturally, to two specific avenues in particular: the pragmatic and the hermeneutical. Indeed, for Alexander, Weber pushed historical and sociological analysis into the obligatory path of the hermeneutics of texts – particularly, of course, religious and legal texts, which are the two traditional sources on which hermeneutics has established both its practice and its theory of interpretation.[9] The extension of Weberian analysis will thus have to deepen a hermeneutics of social life (anchored in the epistemological perspective of "post-positivism" defended by Alexander). But the problematic of sociology opening up to questions concerning the meaning of action and social order is just as much about looking at the contemporary conditions of their realization. In this context, Alexander will draw his references from pragmatism (and its variants stemming from ethnomethodology and symbolic interactionism) – and rightly so, since it is a matter of having a grip on contemporary reality, not just its historical background. Let's recall that Weber conceived the analysis of the meaning of action as a function of the meaning attributed to actions by social actors themselves (Weber 1978: 4). However, the great paradox of this sociology was to deprive itself of basic theoretical resources in order to reach these ends – either in social psychology, for example, or in an empirical sociological method that manages to lean on the analysis of the meanings proposed by the social actors themselves.[10]

The American sociological tradition that emerged from pragmatism has been quite fertile, producing several analytical currents that rely on a sociological analysis empirically oriented towards individual meanings produced in particular contexts. The first of these currents retained by Alexander is symbolic interactionism, defined by Herbert Blumer (1969), who displays a filiation to George Herbert Mead's pragmatism but emphasizes the inter-individual character of action within what he calls a "unit act."

Meaning is here produced in a context of interaction where
at least two individuals meet, which is problematic in several
respects, and even for Blumer's claimed Meadian filiation, as
Alexander (1987: 218–22) rightly points out.[11] The emphasis
on meaning that points unilaterally to the individualistic (or
inter-individual) dimension thus appears deeply problematic
to Alexander, since it obliterates any reference to the social
order as constituting the obligatory background of such
an inscription of meaningful action. Another variant of
this symbolic interactionism is found in Erving Goffman,
whose individualistic and "strategic" analyses of social life
Alexander also criticizes. Noting in passing that Goffman
insists more than Blumer on the belonging of individuals
to the social order, through the Durkheimian inflection
highlighting rituals and performances in which the actors
in a situation engage, Alexander considers nevertheless that
the Goffmanian "presentation of self" does not succeed in
finally rising beyond the horizon of individual interactions,
in a consequent thematization of the social order (Alexander
1987: 230–7).[12] But the current that attracted Alexander's
attention even more is the ethnomethodology developed by
Harold Garfinkel, and the reason for this is that the latter is
in fact more closely linked, at least at the beginning, to an
immanent critique of Parsons, since he was his student. Indeed,
from a combination of Parsonian theory and phenomenology
(Edmund Husserl, and especially Alfred Schütz (1967)),
Garfinkel manages to establish an analysis of individual
action that seeks to show how one maintains an ambivalent
relation to the social order by confronting it at the level of
the presuppositions of the social relations it seeks to exhibit,
while managing to contradict it in the rearrangement of the
"indexical" activities it sets up (Alexander 1987: 257–80).
For Garfinkel, the production of meaning is unproblematic
when it remains unquestioned because it is attached to a
routine order, but the real analytical task of what will become
ethnomethodology is precisely to suspend credit in relation to
this routine order by questioning the way in which the actors
produce it, according to characteristics that can be identified
empirically (by their "indexicality") in the interaction situations themselves.[13] But this suspension of the routine order,
and ultimately the very production of this normative order, is

in the end the sole responsibility of the actors, and this poses a problem for Alexander from an analytical point of view.[14] The problem with all these approaches stemming more or less directly from pragmatism and seeking to localize meaning on the level of social interactions is that they remain too individualistic. They are thus incapable of grasping elements relating to the social order other than by assimilating them to autonomous constructions on the part of individuals, if not completely independently with respect to the general social order in which they are inscribed.

The hermeneutic approach allows us to go beyond these limitations because, by insisting on the relation of the part to the whole, it spontaneously situates individual action in relation to the normative social order. Alexander's first substantial formulation of cultural sociology introduced in *Twenty Lectures: Sociological Theory Since World War II* (1987) poses this explicit relationship between hermeneutics and cultural sociology (as we saw in chapter 1), and thus directly takes up the questions left unanswered by Weber by approaching them in a partial way through the perspectives stemming from pragmatism.[15] The hermeneutics in question here was rooted in the perspective explicitly developed by Dilthey for the program of the sciences of the mind (*Geisteswissenschaften*), parallel to the sciences of culture (*Kulturwissenschaften*) that inspired Weber. This transfer of a "method" previously applied in the study of legal and theological documents to the enlarged field of "texts," in a very broad sense from poetry to philosophy, was able to be applied to fields as diverse as economics or artistic practice.[16] With the support of developments from symbolic anthropology, particularly from Clifford Geertz and Paul Ricœur – in his essays on the expanded reference of textuality to social action – hermeneutics became an important component of cultural sociology, to the point where it was proposed, as we have seen, as a main principle of the "strong program" in its version of "structural hermeneutics."[17] Dilthey formed his initial definition of hermeneutics through an understanding of subjective experience, which he did not limit to any particular type of action; instead he opened it up to all its dimensions, situating individuality in its expanded relationship to personal, social, historical, and cultural context. He refers to "mind," which touches all these domains, and at the same time it joins individual subjectivity and its social environment – this brings Dilthey close to Hegelian philosophy. Alexander takes note of this opening, which makes it possible to challenge the exclusivity Weber gives to instrumental action while bringing Dilthey closer to Geertz, who envisages considering all subjectivity precisely from the fabric of relations established within a "cultural system" (Alexander 1987: 287–91). As a former student of Parsons, Geertz delved into the question of interpretation by attempting to overcome functionalist rigidity. He expanded out to include culture in its own right, without its being subjected to constraints linked to integration in the "social system," thus reversing the typical order of priority. Because of the autonomy of culture, in its inventive and creative capacity, the social order takes on a specific and dense consistency – as Geertz shows when he analyzes his famous example of Balinese cockfighting, and as he more broadly envisions when treating ideology and religion as "cultural systems" (Geertz 1973, 1983). For Alexander, Geertz's inter-pretive approach, which resolutely insists on the precedence of the "cultural system" over all other determinations, has the advantage of leaving behind the demands of considering action in relation to "values" rather than symbols while maintaining a multidimensional perspective (Alexander 1987: 306–7). What makes Geertz's proposals valuable is that, while maintaining the autonomy of culture and the presence of strong symbolic structures (as does the structuralism of Saussure and Lévi-Strauss), they deploy analytical principles that go beyond a simple "idealism" (as in Durkheim) in their interpretation of social life. It is indeed *symbolic action* that becomes the heart of the analysis, thus linking meaning to both individual action and the social order. For Alexander, Geertz's piece "Ideology as a Cultural System" (1973: 193–233) best manages to characterize this analytical orientation, exemplifying a hermeneutic that does not simply hold analysis in the Diltheyan sense or express a textuality situated in abstraction of the possibility of action towards it. In fact, according to Alexander, Geertz succeeded in shifting the philosophy of consciousness, on which Dilthey's herme-neutics still relied, to the philosophy of language that marked the landscape of philosophy in the twentieth century. Thus, from the point of view of the discourses perceived through the lens of symbolic action, cultural sociology can undertake its own hermeneutic while situating symbolic action in relation to the political, which calls for a new theorization. As such, the "civil sphere" becomes the meeting place for symbolic action and the normative cultural order, according to an analytical perspective able to show the symbolic depth of a moral "codification" of meaning, anchored in a register of background code where links to the religious depth of their origins are discovered.

The civil sphere and political debates: reconstruction of civil religion

Invoking "civil religion" to describe the civil sphere that Alexander theorized seems to be a useful way of presenting things, especially since support for such a view is provided by Robert N. Bellah (1978), who made it a principal theme of his research following the distance he took from his teacher Parsons. Bellah is important to Alexander for the same reasons as Geertz: for the ability to consider the autonomy of culture and its necessary relation to individual action, while maintaining the potential for a multidimensional analysis in contrast to the rigidity of Parsonian functionalism. Moreover, by making this idea of "civil religion" his focus, Bellah concretized in sociology what Geertz had done for anthropology (Alexander 1987: 306–12; Alexander and Sherwood 2002).[18] When de Tocqueville coined the notion of "civil religion" in *Democracy in America* ([1835] 2004), it had initiated a reflection on the profound symbolic transformations taking place in the wake of mass democracy with the abandonment of traditional religion as the basis of social life and the establishment of completely autonomous political institutions.[19] In retrospect, the whole role played by religion within politics, as Weber and Durkheim had been able to foresee, became the site of such fusion of the two domains, but whose redefinition opened the way to all sorts of possibilities, including the well-known "polytheism of values."[20] The inflection Alexander gave to this notion of "civil religion" in his theorization of the *civil sphere* resolutely extended these analyses, which would become central for cultural sociology: that of democracy and citizen participation, both of which must hold to a symbolic register capable of binding the religious and the political.

To this theoretical consideration we must add a socio-historical contextualization of a more *ideological* nature. This awareness came at the very moment of the affirmation of a "new world order" (the expression proclaimed by George Bush Sr in 1989), which appeared following the collapse of the Soviet Union, the fall of the Berlin Wall, and the horizons that seem to be opening up for civil society on a global level. Alexander considers these political events in a text where he notes sociology's lack of an adequate theorization of democracy (Alexander 1991a, 1991b). This text seems programmatic in several respects, and its title, "Bringing Democracy Back In: Universalistic Solidarity and the Civil Sphere," appears to determine the direction of the many social analyses that will unfold within cultural sociology.

The civil society discovered in this way acquires an exceptional significance in that it is situated as an entity not directly linked to the existence of the state; in Alexander's eyes it exists before the state, while at the same time it could not simply be reduced to the requirements of state structures in terms of the absolute power they would represent. Alexander wants to reposition, in the sense he gives to the "civil sphere," a tradition of political analysis very well established within Western thought – particularly since Hegel's *Philosophy of Right* – which makes the existence of the state (or its equivalents in the ancient *polis* or in the ferments of modern thought), plus the monopoly of power and violence it embodies, the center of political action. According to Alexander (1991a), sociology must acknowledge the "rich and thick existence of society beneath and outside of the State" which possesses the characteristics inherent in a form of universalism supporting a wider citizen solidarity through its values.[21] The "civil sphere" becomes here the analytical anchor point par excellence, because it represents the confluence of all dimensions of social life.[22]

Cultural sociology rapidly incorporated this thematic, which would eventually be more completely theorized into a whole analytic program.[23] In 1993, a few years before the "strong program" was declared, Jeffrey Alexander and Philip Smith proposed centering the endeavor in this direction. It would be a question of giving systematic form to the analysis of the "discourse of civil society" (Alexander 1992a) according to a perspective capable of synthesizing post-Parsonian approaches, symbolic anthropology, the advances of semiotics, post-structuralism, hermeneutics, and Durkheim's mature position on religious sociology. The challenge was to grasp the symbolic reality of the discourses and actions that are played out on the political scene, assuming that "[p]eople, groups, nations, understand their progress through time in terms of stories, plots which have beginnings, middles and ends, heroes and antiheroes, epiphanies and denouements, dramatic, comic and tragic forms," and by situating what the social sciences have generally ignored: that it is a question of the "mythical dimension of even the most secular societies" (Alexander and Smith 1993: 156).[24] In particular, it is a question of identifying the codes that structure the cultural existence of societies and the way in which these are articulated with social structures, through the phenomenon of institutionalization, according to a logic open to the recognition of situations, struggles, and functional imperatives (ibid.: 160). The codification of political discourse and action is structured according to binary oppositions that refer, for example, to either "democratic" or "undemocratic," touching the classification of political orientations according to a "grammar" structured by the cultural tradition in question. This structure of the discourse of civil society is not reducible to only one "discourse," because it crosses numerous other discourses of diverse, opposed, and even contradictory origins. Nevertheless, it constitutes a basic reference for public debates that occur in "times of tension, unease, and crisis" (ibid.: 166). Examples of this dynamic of cultural forms, which become case studies for analysis, are drawn from the American experience – such as the crises that shook the institution of the American presidency in the nineteenth century, notably concerning Ulysses S. Grant, or Richard Nixon in the twentieth century, as seen earlier in Alexander's analysis.

For Alexander, the challenge is clear and (relatively) simple: to achieve "a model of democratic societies that pays more attention to solidarity and social values – to what and how people speak, think and feel about politics" (Alexander 1997: 115–16). While the political experience of the twentieth century has made it possible to grasp some of the limits of democratic systems, and criticism – especially Marxist criticism – has eloquently testified to this, modern political thought (from Hobbes to Hegel, Montesquieu, and Madison) and contemporary forms (from Michael Walzer to Luc Boltanski and Laurent Thévenot, Alain Touraine, and Charles Taylor) still allow us to set down benchmarks that define an adequate theorizing horizon. Alexander's book *The Civil Sphere*, published in 2006, synthesizes all of these views and allows us to glimpse the analytical continuation that is still opening up for cultural sociology.

In this imposing work of nearly 800 pages, which can be considered to be a "response" to the model of public sphere elaborated by Habermas through his theory of communicative action (as we saw at the end of the previous chapter), Alexander puts forward a theory that allows him to describe: 1) the structures and dynamics of the civil sphere, while paying attention to 2) the social movements that work on it from the inside and questioning 3) the "modes of incorporation" that are proper to it. These are indeed the three main fundamental axes according to which the theorization of the civil sphere is presented, and which will in fact constitute the main analytical axes according to which cultural sociology will develop. As the next two chapters will consider these developments, I will present here only the main intentions for elaborating a *concept* likely to foster a commitment to a "common secular faith" inscribed in a social solidarity that aims for justice in the treatment of all its members. By presenting this concept from the point of view of a science that wants to be both normative and empirical, one that that is open to a multidimensional and reflexive sociological practice, it is largely a question of considering the constitution of this civil sphere as a real project for contemporary society (Alexander 2006: 3–9).

Alexander places this project of the civil sphere into the position of a sociology which, while holding to its scientific and "post-positivist" orientation, refutes the scientistic reduction to an empiricism without theory, or to a

merely "abstract" or "utopian" vision. Adding a hermeneutic influence (from Dilthey, Ricœur, and Gadamer) that
aims to make the category of reason an experience not so
much transcendental as practical, integrated with personal
experience according to its own sociohistorical horizon, he
reiterates the possibility of an analysis attached to "reason"
more broadly understood, thus directly contravening the
Weberian diagnosis.[25] He is committed to making sociological
analysis a reflexive practice that can link the particular and
the universal – the proposal of a true concept that appears,
on the one hand, to be logically founded and, on the other,
allows an escape from the relativism that often overwhelms
contemporary modes of thought. The dialectic inherent in the
experience of reason in the world, which has more recently
critically judged modernity (and after it had been properly
"sanctified" in the previous period), must prevail if one
wants to reach a judgment capable of recognizing both the
successes and failures of this socio-historical development.
In other words, it is a question of recognizing the legacy of
the Enlightenment and its aftermath in the progress of the
contemporary world as much as the legacy of the nihilism
resulting from the catastrophes that led this same world to its
regressions, such as the Holocaust in particular.[26]

In this context, the theorization of the "civil sphere" is
Alexander's answer to Weber's pessimistic diagnosis and
the specific analytic that will make it possible to deal with
questions concerning the fate of modernity within contemporary society. And it is to this task that Alexander will
devote himself with the extensions of cultural sociology,
which he will draw in particular from Parsons's critique, as
we will see in the next chapter.

5

The Civil Sphere and the "Societal Community": Beyond Parsons

The concept of the *civil sphere* presented briefly in the previous chapter must be contextualized in the overall project of Alexander's cultural sociology; it must also be situated first and foremost in its relation to the sociology of Talcott Parsons. Indeed, Alexander's entire enterprise has been situated from the very beginning in an agonistic relationship with Parsons's structuro-functionalism. The first attempts to go beyond this approach in the early 1980s, under the name "neofunctionalism," allow us to see that what was most theoretically important was precisely the refoundation of the Parsonian sociological project, which had been undermined by demands for integration into the social system and homeostatic equilibrium. These were criticisms of Parsons formulated by his former students, in particular Clifford Geertz and Robert N. Bellah, who became allies in the theoretical construction of cultural sociology, and they did not hide their allegiances to Parsons's functionalist colleagues, such as Neil Smelser, Edward Shils, and Shmuel Eisenstadt, who were acknowledged by Alexander in the continuation of his own project. Perhaps it is time to emphasize here the "ecumenical" character of Alexander's approach, which has always been to collaborate with many colleagues in the development of his own sociological project – not without criticism, most of the time, but also inspired by them, marking the contribution of each of them in the development of his own analytical views.[1]

This chapter, which outlines analytical visions derived from developments in cultural sociology, is primarily about this question: how does Alexander's concept of the *civil sphere* as a general analytical framework for contemporary societies really differ from Parsons's sociology, and in particular his concept of the "social system"?

The question is worth asking, especially since, in the course of the development of Alexander's concept of the civil sphere, we also encounter Parsons's later notion of "societal community," which characterizes the development of American society, particularly the conditions whereby the political citizenry participates in the social order.[2] One might thus think that Alexander, at this point in his own theoretical and conceptual elaborations, meets Parsons's views quite directly, although he had tried since the very beginning of his own sociological enterprise to distance himself from them in a critical way, or even attempted to go beyond them by reformulating the "classics" of sociology. But does Alexander's "new classical sociology" really go beyond Parsons? And, if so, how?

In chapter 1, we briefly mentioned the way in which Alexander intended to distance himself from Parsonian sociology, if not from the project of sociology in general, by recalling that the "post-positivist" epistemological position he defended relied more on a so-called *personalized* approach to sociological practice. Similarly, the scientistic attitude of classical sociology (and also, largely, of mainstream sociology) was downplayed, albeit without denying the requirements of universalism and empiricism, which came to constitute core principles of cultural sociology. This *personalized* approach implies a higher degree of reflexivity – that is to say, one that exceeds by uniting the objectivity of sociological analysis and the subjectivity of the person conducting it. This has the effect of directly engaging reflexivity in the development of sociological interpretation (characteristic of a properly hermeneutic approach) rather than relegating the latter only to an "objective" relay of analysis conducted in a strictly impersonal way.[3] The whole experience of knowledge is then integrated into a "practical philosophy" rather than a "scientific practice" (or "scientism"), as it is in the natural sciences. Alexander, in taking the side of reflexivity in socio-logical analysis, thus spontaneously places himself as an opponent of Parsonian positivist objectivism – at least in terms of the epistemological position he takes. One may interpret all the theoretical efforts deployed by cultural sociology in the aftermath of this epistemological stance, especially those appealing to hermeneutics, as moving in this direction. Indeed, the reconceptualization of civil society in the terms of a "civil sphere" aims precisely towards this, especially as it sees itself as an analytical project as much as a conceptual and practical one.[4]

Since the autonomy of culture is the basic postulate of Alexander's vision, and not the requirement of functional integration into a "social system," the theoretical distance with Parsons also seems to be unequivocally established. And yet the question remains of homeostatic equilibrium, which was for Parsons the fundamental motive for the integration of the different systems of action with respect to each other; it is, however, to some extent reformulated by the vision of a civil sphere that fulfills the expectations of the underlying civil religion. This latter concept allows Alexander to bring back Durkheim and Weber's sociologies of religion in terms of ritual and attachment to a sacralized cultural tradition, although he displaces to the side of politics properly theological attachments that weighed down "civil religion" in its classical definition (from de Tocqueville to Bellah). But do we not find here, in the stability of symbolic references linked to a "structural hermeneutics," the persis-tence of a societal equilibrium that is presumed rather than problematized?

The fourth volume of *Theoretical Logic in Sociology*, entitled *The Modern Reconstruction of Classical Thought: Talcott Parsons*, already partly answered this question. In this imposing work, which in a way closes the argument of the "post-positivist" sociology that Alexander wants to advance, Parsons's sociology is examined in great detail, according to its chronological development and different phases, in order to see the disciplinary contributions it has made, as well as its limits concerning the sociological project as such.[5] As already mentioned, Alexander considers the Parsonian synthesis to be one of the classics of sociology, since it seems difficult to see how a return to the classics alone can avoid Parsons's criticisms and synthesis of the fundamental principles and shortcomings he identified in Durkheim, Weber, and Pareto. And in order to allow updates to the synthetic under-standing of *social action*, it is equally necessary to subject Parsons himself to such a critical examination if we want to see what sociology can consist of *after* Parsons, which is already apparent in Alexander's own readings of the classics.[6] Alexander's critique will therefore target the heart of Parsonian sociology, showing where and how it has fallen into a form of positivism that can no longer correspond to the epistemological requirements of a sociology that now makes *interpretation* fundamental to its practice. This criticism will therefore touch upon the "social system," insofar as it repre-sents for Parsons the fundamental element of integration (within the structure of social action schematized by the AGIL). More specifically, Alexander wants to show that, by reducing an initially multidimensional approach (since it combines different functions within a system of exchange between the different subsystems – biological, psychological, social, and cultural), Parsons's fundamental methodological problems can be seen: a unilateral reification of the system of exchange and a conflation of the model with empirical reality (Alexander 1983b: 77–85, 156–62, 174–94). This reduction was initially called for by the degree of complexity reached by Parsons's theory, which strove to produce an analytical refinement capable of grasping social action within human societies. It was also required by the integration of Durkheim and Weber into a socio-historical understanding of the social order, attentive to the ways society evolves to produce specific determinations according to the particular cases that it addresses. For Alexander, Parsons shows great insight by adding the contributions of Freudian psychoanalysis to his understanding of the relations between the psychological development of the personality and the social structures that it has to internalize; this demonstrates the exceptional analytical capacity and versatility of the Parsonian approach, at least in principle. However, according to Alexander, the presuppositions of Parsonian analysis also need to be interrogated according to two main aspects: firstly, these presuppositions feed the idealistic vision of a social system where a version of voluntary individualism prevails that confuses normative order and social action; and, secondly, the privilege given to the economic system in particular freezes a reference to the values ultimately associated with the medium of exchange (money) within the social and cultural system – a position albeit modified by Parsons's later research on the prevalence of other media of influence and commitment to values (Alexander 1983b: 212–76; 2005a: 99). Alexander's concept of the civil sphere will critically counteract these shortcomings by resolutely focusing its analysis on symbolic actions of a political nature, while maintaining the precedence of a symbolic order defined above all by culture and its possibilities of autonomous development.[7]

Parsons had elaborated his concept of "societal community" in the context of a synthesis that he wanted to propose concerning the evolution of societies – particularly of American society, which he situated in a historical (evolutionary) perspective as the apex of human societies (Parsons 1966, 1971, 2007). This optimism largely reflects the historical context of the immediate post-war period as a theoretical synthesis surprisingly in tune with the scientific developments of the time (in biology and cybernetics in particular), as well as a specific ideological dimension. As such, from the 1960s on, Parsonian sociology was an ideal target for criticism, with the rise of the social protest movements (such as the civil rights movement, the critique of American imperialism in the student movement protesting the Vietnam war, etc.) and internal critiques of systemic "grand theory" (from Garfinkel's ethnomethodology to Blumer's symbolic interactionism and Geertz's symbolic anthropology), as well as questions surrounding the overall fit between structuro-functionalism and the realities of contemporary society from an interpretive point of view. Alexander's personal experience as a member of the younger generation challenging virtually every aspect of the Parsonian perspective in the 1960s and 1970s thus provided him with a basis for moving beyond it, though his respect for Parsonian sociology prevented him from completely jettisoning it.[8] Also, it is an overcoming of the Parsonian synthesis illustrated by the concept of "societal community" that Alexander's concept of *civil sphere* aspires to. This is attempted through a dialectical criticism able to offer a new version of this synthesis, predominated by the union of justice (promised in its legal and impersonal forms by society) and integration (ensured in its more personal, affective, and emotional forms, by the community). This new synthesis is much more open to the social tensions that make of the civil sphere an ongoing *search* for "societal community" rather than a simple statement of its existence.[9] Parsons had minimized the tensions, if not the contradictions, feeding the historical development of contemporary society in a simplified ideological vision of modernity and a form of sociological positivism managing to maintain that the process of differentiation was automatically completed by a normative generalization capable of integrating all individuals – without perceiving that this integration always remained only partial, indeed unfair, by relying on values associated with the dominant group in society, thus referring to a "formal" universalism only, blind to the particularistic oppositions that can call it into question (Alexander 2005a: 93, 106–7). For Alexander, it is, rather, a question of agreeing to submit to the analysis of these tensions and contradictions by underlining how they are constitutive of the gap that exists between ideals of social justice, integration, solidarity, and democracy. It is with this perspective that cultural sociology intends to theorize the civil sphere.

At the same time, however, Alexander also chooses to distance himself from the concept of "civil society," which was making a comeback within sociology around 1989–90 (particularly in the ideological context of the New World Order discussed above), just as much as it had informed modern political thought, as well as sociological analysis, virtually since its origins. He thus points out that previous conceptions of civil society are too closely tied to imperatives of constitutions of the modern state and the bourgeois morality that accompanied it, and that cultural sociology requires another conception, localized in a sphere "that can be analytically independent, empirically differentiated, and more morally universalistic vis-à-vis the state and the market and from other social spheres" (Alexander 2006: 31). This new conception of civil society is distinctive because it is constituted above all by solidarity, "in which a certain kind of universalizing community comes to be culturally defined and to some degree institutionally enforced." This solidarity is also "exhibited and sustained by public opinion, deep cultural codes, distinctive organizations – legal, journalistic, and associational – and such historically specific interactional practice as civility, criticism, and mutual respect." While inhabited by ideal norms and principles that aim at justice and democracy, the civil sphere is the site of a solidarity fueled by "codes and narratives, the institutions and the interactions" that "clearly depart from those that regulate the world of economic cooperation and competition, the affectual and intimate relations of family life, and the transcendental and abstract symbolism that form the media of intellectual and religious interaction and exchange" (ibid.: 33). While pursuing its goals of justice and democracy, the civil sphere truly becomes the arena in which the issues that run through our society are played out, for "[t]he universality that is the ambition of this sphere, its demands to be inclusive, to fulfill collective obligations while at the same time protecting individual autonomy," are qualities that have characterized "the court of last resort" of modern and postmodern societies (ibid.: 34). Instead of viewing civil society as the place where promises of emancipation have been systematically flouted, being especially associated with the domination exercised over it by the state (or capitalism), it is rather that the social and cultural movements that run through it allow for the expression of conflict and their possible resolutions, and thus for possible institutional (and constitutional) reforms, according to terms offered to sociological analysis. It is indeed in this direction that cultural sociology's analytical efforts are directed, as it not only characterizes the civil sphere, it does so in accordance with the reflexivity to which it subscribes, to *form* (and *reform*) it according to sociological parameters.[10]

This formation is understood in terms of a real *symbolic structure*, a normative order that comes from a cultural complex belonging to all societies, from which Western society has drawn a typically democratic model, allowing it to maximize the components of social justice, inclusion, and solidarity that fundamentally define it. Alexander's concept of the *civil sphere* explicitly emerges from this perspective:

This symbolic structure, both in its universalist and particularist lines, was already clearly implied in the very first philosophical thinking about democratic societies that emerged in ancient Greece. Since the Renaissance, it has permeated popular thinking and behavior, even while its centrality in philosophical thinking has continued to be sustained. The symbolic structure takes different forms in different nations, and it is the historical residue of diverse movements in social, intellectual and religious life – of classical ideas, republicanism and Protestantism, Enlightenment and liberal thought, of the revolutionary and common law traditions. The cultural implications of these variegated movements, however, have been drawn into a highly generalized symbolic system that divides civic virtue from civic vice in a remarkably stable and consistent way. It is for this reason that, despite divergent historical roots and variations in national elaboration, the language that forms the cultural core of civil society can be isolated as a general structure and studied empirically as a relatively autonomous symbolic form. (Alexander 2000: 298–9)[11]

The civil sphere is thus posited as the sociological conceptualization of this symbolic structure, in that it will analytically examine its different components. This question of the participation of sociology in the formation of the civil sphere is important, since it anticipates the way in which any discourse or symbolic action finds resonance within it. It is true even when these discourses and symbolic actions come from "non-civil" spheres – the family, economy, the state, religion, science, etc. – which function according to different principles, such as unconditional love, profit and competition, the exercise of power, adherence by faith, theoretical and analytical research, etc. The civil sphere thus has its own structure, established on a socio-historical level according to differentiations resulting from modern society and bourgeois democracies, which produced this conception between the subjective or private domain of individuals (often characterized as that of particular "interests") and the objective or public domain of the state institution (often characterized by "reason of state" or the "general interest"). However, contemporary developments have also made this structure more complex through the development of "communicative institutions" (public opinion, mass media, polls, various associations) and "regulative institutions" (voting, the party system, elective offices of representation), which also include the domain of law and legislation (Alexander 2006: 69–192).[12] Although relatively independent of these other spheres of social life, the civil sphere (representing the principles of autonomy, solidarity, justice, and inclusion) is always informed by these other spheres, as their expressions are "translated" by (and possibly also indirectly "bifurcated" into) the civil sphere by one or several elements of its structure. This can create occasions of conflict, which then find resolution through the principles of this civil sphere: this is what motivates social movements, be they labor-based, feminist, anti-racist or antisexist, ecological, religious, etc. (ibid.: 203–9). The porosity of the boundaries of the civil sphere means that it welcomes these expressions of all types, but according to the principles that structure it; this is why the civil sphere finally appears as the "tribunal." As a discourse, sociology also penetrates the civil sphere at levels that can be said to be analytical and conceptual: to focus on the civil sphere at the level of sociological analysis also means to participate in its promotion within its different instances – but particularly in relation to its fundamental principles (democracy, inclusion, solidarity, justice), since sociological analysis itself identifies them and describes their ramifications through social manifestations.

It is thus clear how Alexander intends to distance himself from Parsons's sociology – as well as from the wider sociological project – by developing it according to a specific overall orientation focused on social transformation and references to cultural elements that exceed the requirement of strict integration into a social system defined essentially in terms of its stability.[13] There is indeed a commitment present in the theoretical and analytical deployment staged here, which participates in the dynamics of the civil sphere. Cultural sociology is literally synonymous with the civil sphere in the interpretation of a democratic social life, where the stakes of justice, solidarity, and inclusion are never won in advance but are nevertheless ever present and constantly in play. Analysis is then conducted to highlight the way in which symbolic expressions of the civil sphere are linked to these democratic issues. This is done by paying attention to social movements, and in particular to their mode of expression within the civil sphere, insofar as such social movements have been the main bearers of various claims within the political actuality of our societies, especially over the last two hundred years.

From Parsons to Touraine and beyond: analysis of performative social movements

For Alexander, the shift to the sociology of social movements was partly inspired by the experience of attending Alain Touraine's sociology laboratory at the École des hautes études en sciences sociales in the early 1990s.[14] This shift thus coincided with the new interest in civil society, and it was important in more than one respect because it provided an opportunity for more precise articulation between the analysis of "discourses of civil society" and analyses to come based on the "performance" of social actors (Alexander and Smith 1993; Alexander 2004a, 2004b, 2004c; Alexander et al. 2006). Thus Alexander will explain this preoccupation with social movements according to a perspective that reinstates the role of the "social actor," as Touraine had thematized it in the 1980s, in the wake of his "sociology of action" of the 1960s (itself a reversal of the Parsonian vision of "social action"). Touraine had already allowed this new interest in civil society to be defined by moving towards the development of a problematic associated with the rise of post-industrial society, centered on information and the place of new claims in the social space with a view to political reforms. He placed it outside the space of the old struggles and the world of work by combining the interests linked to "information society," where subjective identity, feminism, consumption, ecology, etc., all seem to point towards a larger cultural transformation. Consequently, this transformation is complex and multifaceted; even if Touraine managed to define some of its contours, he doesn't manage to provide a unified analysis that is convincing from a global point of view. Thus, we do not find in Touraine a "hermeneutic reconstruction" of each of these various ideological expressions that would allow us to consider them as part of an overall political and cultural movement, if not in terms of a transposition into the old forms of opposition to the state. This allows Alexander to make civil society the result of these various expressions rather than their cause or origin (Alexander 1996b). Such a move is illustrated by the evolution of Touraine's thinking in the early 1990s, when he expressed more pessimistic views on democracy and modernity in works that were increasingly focused on the question of individual subjectivity. Here, Alexander points out that any hope, both practical and analytical, for the collective seemed to definitively fade away in favor of a disenchanted return to the stale positions of classical sociology – close to a vision of the anomic society outlined especially by Durkheim, to whom Alexander explicitly compares him.[15] At this point, the effort of theorization, allied to a change of analytical register, must come into play to bring out the potentiality of the civil sphere to draw from structures and values to restore its capacity to act in the constitution of society.[16] Whereas the bourgeois revolutions had to face the structures of the *ancien régime*, the question for contemporary (mass) democracies is, rather, to harken back to the principles established by modern societies to reactualize what constitutes their new symbolic bases. As such, the social movements must present themselves as exemplary representatives of "the sacred values, as the bearers of social, national and even primordial myths, as cultural innovators who can create new norms and new institutions that will allow resources to be channelled in different ways" (Alexander 1996b: 225). In brief:

> The power of such movements depends in the first instance less on organizational command and networks of exchange than on subjective commitments of loyalty and solidarity. Such commitments can be produced only when social movements create and sustain new forms of meaning and more attractive forms of personal and group identity. (Ibid.)

This perspective is present in Alexander's treatment of three issues that have crossed the horizon of American society in recent decades, revealing the full potential of the civil sphere and affecting its capacity for political reformism aimed at social restorative justice: feminism, civil rights, and the integration of Jewish identity in the United States. I will focus briefly here on the first two in order to give a sense of the kind of analysis produced by cultural sociology, reserving the treatment of the third for later because of its connection to the Holocaust and its specificity in terms of the kind of universalism it involves.

The question of feminism is posed in Alexander's eyes according to the unfolding of the social movement that has carried it, from its first lineaments in the context of the bourgeois revolutions (French and American) at the end of the eighteenth century, when the principles of women's equality were first enunciated (by Mary Wollstonecraft in particular), to the more recent third-wave feminist demands from the 1990s onwards (Alexander 2006: 235, 263). The social movement developed from its beginnings with the suffragettes in the nineteenth century, to the institutionalization of political reforms resulting in women's full citizenship (among others in the 19th Amendment to the US Constitution, adopted in 1920, concerning the right to vote), to the second- and third-wave feminisms of the 1960s and 1990s. What we are witnessing here is a social and cultural transformation for which the civil sphere is "responsible," insofar as it welcomed the debates that animated the different protagonists, the categorical oppositions that comprised the core struggle, and finally the resolutions of these tensions offered through the changes claimed and carried out. From the point of view of the civil sphere, the social struggles leading to societal transformation are, however, presented more as an actualization of the potentialities of justice that this civil sphere conceals in itself, as Alexander underlines:

> The categorical divisions of the civil sphere have been stable for centuries, but the signifieds of these civil and anticivil signifiers certainly have not. In one historical period, differences of gender, class, race, religion, and sexuality are taken to be primordial differences and criticized or sentimentalized as anticivil by the groups that organize and represent the civil core. At a later historical time, such supposedly natural qualities are seen merely as "constructed," as are the once invisibly primordial qualities that had, up until that time,

defined the distinctiveness of civil society's core group. Reflexivity is not about changing the categories that define the civil sphere; it is about learning how they can be instantiated in a new ways. (Ibid.: 263).

The dialectic inherent to the civil sphere seems to find its balance here; once movement is realized, the civil sphere, by its own virtualities, allows these feminist social transformations to be carried out through different channels.[17] The analysis that unfolds in this respect is multidimensional, showing how the different structures of the civil sphere act at one moment or another in this overall dynamic (social actors discussing these themes, open demonstrations and mass mobilizations, the media reporting on these demonstrations and transferring these issues to a wider social plane, political processes involving voting, representation, and institutions in the development of legislation, etc.). Although linked to the civil sphere, the wider political issue is a redefinition of the social status of women (i.e. the question of gender), which affects other social spheres, such as the world of work and the family in particular, but just as much the male world in general, since this is obviously redefined in a reciprocal manner to the changes that fundamentally affect gender status. A whole project of symbolic (re)codification is at play, which according to different scales interacts with the three waves of feminism, postponing of course the questions that always arise regarding claims of equality; although transformations have occurred in many domains, it has not yet entirely succeeded (as seen in contemporary movements such as #MeToo – Alexander 2019: 73–110).

The same might be said about the civil rights movement in the United States, according to the specific motivations that marked the demand for equality on the part of the African-American community between the official abolition of slavery in 1865 through the 13th Amendment to the US Constitution, following the Civil War, and the adoption of the Civil Rights Act of 1964 and beyond (Alexander 2006: 265–391).[18] In this regard, Alexander once again deploys a multidimensional analysis that takes into account the social movement initiated at the beginning of the twentieth century by the National Association for the Advancement of Colored People (NAACP) to fight against the discriminatory ("Jim Crow") laws instituted in certain Southern states to perversely counter the effects of abolition.[19] He shows how this movement gradually took shape until the 1950s with the rising figure of Martin Luther King Jr, a figure who would become emblematic (or *iconic*, in Alexander's terminology) as public protests and arrests spread throughout the South, leading to the general mobilization of American public opinion. Again, here, the discourse and actions within the civil rights movement – relayed by the media and public opinion, and then by the state apparatus and finally legislation – are the focus of the analysis, as the dynamics at work within various structures of the civil sphere are seen as a complex dialectic through which restorative justice points the way. But this occurred only to a certain extent, since, as in the case of feminism, the civil rights movement did not entirely resolve the question of racial discrimination, socially speaking, nor was it able to prevent more radical African-American groups (such as the Black Panther movement, with the emblematic figure of Malcolm X) from pursuing demands through other channels (Alexander 2006: 390–1).[20]

In this expression of social movements within the civil sphere, new symbolic codifications of oppositions appear (sacred/profane, pure/impure, participative/exclusive, voluntary/authoritarian, rigid/flexible, etc.) whose purpose, beyond the particular situation that they put in play, is to universalize their claims and establish new frameworks of practices that join the whole of society – according to the Hegelian model of the "universal becoming concrete" (Alexander 1996b: 227).[21] This implies a set of rhetorical strategies and symbolic actions that, through their appeals to fundamental structures, can transform the social order through culture. This turn to the performative, to the theatricality of the civil sphere, is an important moment in cultural sociology – a necessary complement to earlier developments that provided the means to rethink the autonomy of culture by ensuring a central reference to the ways in which symbolization is challenged (Alexander 2003, 2004a, 2004b, 2017a).

Cultural pragmatics and the challenges of symbolic codification

Alexander identifies the link between the civil sphere and the performativity of symbolic action as inherent in the emergence of the "social drama" enacted in every society, from the most archaic to the most contemporary – with, of course, differences in the symbolic forms involved that range, for example, "from ritual to theater" (to use the title of a book by Victor Turner (1982), on whom Alexander partly bases his analyses). This is not without a critical revision of those theses that, from Turner to Richard Schechner (2003), have marked the analyses of "performance studies" in the contemporary context (Alexander 2004a: 544–5).[22] In order to show how the origin of the civil sphere, as well as its evolution, are in a contiguous relationship with the way in which symbolic actions are represented and manifested within the cultural order, Alexander underlines that this is inescapable if one wants to access the meaning of *cultural pragmatics* implied in the analytical approach of cultural sociology, since it is there in particular that the "power of representation" rubs shoulders with the "representation of power" in an agonistic relationship. It is indeed a crucial point of argumentation, especially if we consider that, according to this model, Parsonian sociology will be definitively left behind by the advances of cultural sociology. Following this, the hermeneutic interpretation will be deployed (according to a statement of the binary oppositions of logic or a structural hermeneutics), finally leading to the analysis of social life through the lens of cultural sociology.

Parsons had considered the question of symbolic formation from the point of view of cybernetic theory and the hierarchy it implies, in which a system with a high degree of organization, and therefore high entropy but low energy, took precedence over a system with a high degree of energy but little organization. This is what allowed him to suggest that the cultural system, where societal values are housed, possessed a greater stability than the biological system (as well as the personality and social systems in the interconnection these represent through the cybernetic hierarchy – a convincing example of which is the channeling of a child's development through the requirements of socialization).[23] Alexander had well perceived this problem of reification of cybernetic theory and its assimilation into the social world in the interpretation of Parsonian sociology (Alexander 1983b). All the subsequent "codification" carried out according to the media of exchange within the subsystems of action (as, for example, money at the level of the economic system, power in the political system, and influence in the social system) thus becomes a way of grasping how the reduction of meaning in social action according to a cybernetic logic acts in the selection of binary oppositions at the level of social action (universal/particular, material/ideal, etc.). This leads to a so-called modal understanding of the possibilities of meaning (according to "pattern variables"), considerably reducing the scope of the proposed sociological interpretation (ibid.: 254–65). As we have already mentioned, Alexander instead presents his own version of symbolic action by way of linguistics, still according to a register of binary oppositions, but this time according to a "structural hermeneutics." Here, the codification operates by means of reference to the background symbolic structures which found their signification.[24] This codification is then a matter of a categorization manifest on a performative level through the representation of symbolic action:

> As constructed by the performative imagination, the background and foreground symbols are structured by codes that provide analogies and antipathies and by narratives that provide chronologies. In symbolizing actors' and audiences' worlds, these narratives and codes simultaneously condense and elaborate, and they imply a wide range of rhetorical devices, from metaphor to synecdoche, to configure social and emotional life in compelling and coherent ways. Systems of collective representations range from "time immemorial" myths to invented traditions created right on the spot, from oral traditions to scripts prepared by such specialists as playwrights, journalists, and speech writers. (Alexander 2004a: 530)

I have already underlined the paradoxical character of this structural hermeneutics when articulated through a reference

to civil religion, for example, translating only the reproduction of fixed cultural symbols. In fact, when one considers
it from this point of view, it seems to me that hermeneutics
would have an advantage to be understood from the point
of view of the *dialectic* that it implies – that is to say, of
the symbolic transformations that take place through the
diachronic course of their manifestations. Here, the proposed
linguistic model refers back to Mikhaïl Bakhtin (1982) and
Valentin N. Voloshinov (1986) in their attempt to break with
the static or synchronic character of Saussurean linguistics,
inspired by the study of language within living interactions
that focuses on its diachronic character. The resulting *dialectical* hermeneutic, by counting on the transformations which
take place in the transpositions from one time to another
(according to Bakhtin's vision of the chronotope), makes it
possible to show not only how codes vary from one time
to another but also how the symbolic structures themselves
end up being transformed. A paradigmatic example of this is
the evolution of citizenship over the last two hundred years,
which has been relieved of its obligatory relationship to
private property as in bourgeois democracies. It has gradually
undergone an unlimited enlargement so that, in mass democracies, it includes every individual as a free and autonomous
person in principle, or formally – which was obviously not
the case in the previous bourgeois democratic regime. In this
spirit, dialectical hermeneutics aims at considering cultural
traditions as dialogues through which symbolic structures
are mobilized in the context of their *reconstruction*. As such,
it relies on ruptures of meaning that make cultural traditions relatively foreign to us, or at least relatively difficult
to spontaneously recognize; this requires an exercise that
attempts to locate their "strangeness" and eventually brings
us back to a "fusion of horizons," according to Hans-Georg
Gadamer (1989). But this is not the method of cultural
sociology, and Alexander's adoption of a *structural* rather
than a dialectical hermeneutics, while it seems to me to pose
some problems, does not prevent him from thinking that it
is possible to analytically describe the mechanisms that take
place within the civil sphere. Some of these mechanisms
touch upon fundamental issues for social integration and
the citizen's capacity to assert a fully democratic demand

for social justice from the point of view of restorative justice (called "civil repair" in this context). This is the relationship, also dialectical in nature, between universalism and particularism as it appears in its manifestations within the civil sphere.[25]

This requirement is thus manifest in terms of a cultural pragmatics allied to performativity according to the different modalities offered by socio-historical circumstances – as we have seen above with the feminist and civil rights movements. But it also counts on a "dramaturgy" that contextualizes scenarios associated with a cultural tradition whose essence belongs to the codification of the civil sphere (and the binary oppositions which constitute it). These performances, inscribed in the present, "innovate, create, and struggle for social change through small but significant revisions of familiar scripts, which are themselves carved from deeply rooted cultural texts." The analyses that emerge show how "the imagined past weighs heavily on the present," but equally that "actors are shown to be capable of lacing the coded past with significant, at times profoundly dramatic revisions" (Alexander et al. 2006: 15). The resulting analyses thus emphasize the ways in which forms of symbolic representation are defined that highlight the struggles through which themes appear within social life. These themes are subsequently perceived through reference to their codification, allowing them to be situated on one side or the other of the civil sphere, and then finally put into play in the political arena in order to effect social transformation. It is always possible that such performances fail in their attempt to transform the normative order, and the dynamics in question in fact count on the possibility that the hoped-for "fusion" with the public is not consummated, but this is the same as in any other dramaturgical or aesthetic expression: they manage, or not, to create a "cathartic" movement whose repercussions are felt through the whole civil sphere.[26] The emphasis on the process of "fusion" between the performance and the audience, which allows for cathartic recognition (and thus plays an important role in restorative justice, insofar as what is staged acquires an institutional status), also brings into play the opposite possibility of "de-fusion," where the performance does not adequately reach the audience and thus fails with respect to what it is trying to convey. In fact, the evolution of contemporary society, particularly its process of differentiation, prevents a complete or satisfactory ritualistic and performative "fusion" from being achieved. Because contemporary society is initially "de-fused," due to its internal dynamics of differentiation, it is only through a performance taking on the status of a unifying ritual that allows for "re-fusion" on the political and social level. But how and why can performances claim this cathartic status? This is where a theory of social and cultural trauma comes into play, which Alexander developed alongside his analyses of cultural pragmatics.

Social and cultural trauma theory: social claims of identity

The fundamental criterion for discerning the value of a political and cultural performance, as Alexander understands it, is that of *authenticity*; when a performance makes it possible both to recognize the adherence of the actors to a specific symbolic expression on the aesthetic level and then to elicit the moral adherence from the public, it achieves an effective "re-fusion."[27] But since this process involves specific situations, it is necessary to consider what, precisely, can make a performance likely to gain public acceptance on the political, social, and especially moral levels. Alexander has proposed a theorization of social and cultural trauma that makes it possible to analyze the conditions under which symbolic expressions in the civil sphere become not only "presentable" but also "universalizable" (Alexander et al. 2004; Eyerman et al. 2011; Alexander 2012a, 2019). The fundamental idea that emerges from this theorization is that a *traumatic* event, whether personal, social, cultural, or historical, does not possess this meaning in itself but, rather, acquires it within a social process of representation – and of course of the performative manifestation of this representation according to determined aesthetic and moral conditions. The usual conceptions of trauma tend to consider the traumatic nature of an event as such – that is to say, as a result of the event itself. For Alexander, more specialized thinking considers trauma in terms of the abrupt change it represents on an individual or social level, or by situating it psychoanalytically on the level of unconscious emotional shock and the defense mechanisms put in place to avoid or circumvent it. Psychoanalysis thus emphasizes this meaning with symbolic character and establishes the link with the possibility of the narration, in the psychoanalytical cure, as a way of facing this unconscious trauma (Alexander 2012a: 6–15). The more sociological analysis, on the other hand, is concerned with the whole social process involved in the meaning an event acquires in order to define its traumatic significance.

The paradigmatic example in this framework is that of the Holocaust, and this is in fact the third case examined within the transformations of the contemporary civil sphere (Alexander 2006: 503–47). This example builds on the social exclusion that Jewish communities have faced throughout history, from the first manifestations of anti-Semitism in the European Middle Ages and into the development of various European nationalities, an exclusion that has been repeated in the United States with regard to Jewish immigration since the end of the nineteenth century, leading to various forms of ostracism. However, the circumstances of the Jewish community's integration into American society were largely shaped by the historical experience of World War II and the aftermath of the Holocaust, which led to a new symbolic configuration constructed through the categorical opposition to Nazism and its evil practices culminating in that tragedy. Unlike the other two examples, of feminism and the civil rights movement, however, the case of the Holocaust is not so much a social movement as a gradual realization of its meaning in a universalized form. As Alexander points out:

> How does a specific and situated historical event, an event marked by ethnic and racial hatred, violence, and war, become transformed into a generalized symbol of human suffering and moral evil, a universalized symbol whose very existence has created historically unprecedented opportunities for ethnic, racial, and religious justice, for mutual recognition, and global conflicts becoming regulated in a more civil way? This cultural transformation has been achieved because the

originating historical event, traumatic in the extreme for a delimited particular group, has come over the last sixty years to be redefined as a traumatic event for all of humankind. Now free-floating rather than situated – universal rather than particular – this traumatic event vividly "lives" in the memories of contemporaries whose parents and grandparents never felt themselves even remotely related to it. (Alexander 2012a: 31)

The universal significance acquired by the Holocaust is thus presented as being constructed gradually, according to the expressions that "move" it from its base in the horrors initially established by Nazism, the genocidal mass elimination that followed, the subsequent stages of recognition of this crime by the Nuremberg trials, the reflection of intellectuals (such as Hannah Arendt), the creation of the state of Israel, and then the books, films, television series, etc., that amplified its meaning in public opinion. In the United States, the Holocaust was thus carried by a whole series of manifestations that reconfigured its meaning in different ways, and from the 1950s to the 1980s this led to the establishment of greater solidarity with the Jewish community within the civil sphere. The various moments of this transformation evoked by Alexander thus situate the particularity of the Holocaust in the relationship it gradually inscribes with a universality that it comes to signify on both national and international level. Despite the interpretations the Holocaust has acquired in certain contexts, particularly surrounding the explicit counterpart of the Palestinian *Nakba* (the "catastrophe") of 1948, for Alexander this event is an illustration of a universal symbol reverberating with social and cultural trauma, a political situation still full of tensions and still to this day unresolved.[28] This example also shows, however, that the universality of the meanings attributed to a political event is never completely closed, and likely to be called into question according to the political conjunctures that animate the civil sphere. Thus, other cases examined by Alexander, such as the Nanjing massacre perpetrated by the Japanese army in China in 1937 or the partition of India and Pakistan in 1947, are also occasion for debates about their significance – either affirmed or invalidated in their deep symbolic value, fundamentally but possibly contradictorily, for the societies involved (Alexander 2012a: 118–54). This opening up of the analytical possibilities offered by social and cultural trauma, which play out within the public sphere, does, however, itself carry its own "universal" theoretical force, allowing Alexander to consider both American and international situations. The problematic of the civil sphere can be used, for example, to analyze the Arab Spring of 2011 and any significant social conflict that shakes societies, from Latin America to Asia and beyond.[29]

It can thus be said that, on the whole, Alexander's cultural sociology has freed itself from Parsons, because it has proposed a change of register on the analytical level. Through the theory of the civil sphere, it attempts to highlight the political transformations contemporary societies are undergoing through an analysis of traumatic issues in the formation of the symbolic order on which these societies are based. In addition, it emphasizes the narrative and performative expressions through which various social actors appear and manifest themselves. One might say that a good part of its orientation is setting up a problematic where the power of representation and the representation of power confront each other. This is what we will examine in the next chapter.

Let us remember, however, that, from the point of view of cultural sociology, this analysis of the civil sphere renews the debate over modernity within our societies by reviving the idea that a strong political dynamic is still the driving force of current societal development, nationally and internationally. If the "trial" of modernity continues to unfold within postmodern societies, this is because they have pursued a historical evolution marked by inflections that sociology (Parsonian in particular) was unable to adequately analyze. It is thus particularly at the level of *representation* that these questions find an answer in cultural sociology, as we will see in Alexander's deepening analyses on this question.

6

The Power of Representation and the Representation of Power

Alexander's cultural sociology proposes a conceptualization new to sociology, an attempt to renew analytical activity in the discipline by centering its own reflexivity and a commitment to what could broadly be called a "democratic culture." This commitment and reflexivity thus presupposes that sociological analysis is itself a stakeholder in the debates and issues that run through the civil sphere, but taking into account the fact, as mentioned before, that its own theorizing effort is accomplished in the very shaping of this civil sphere and in its capacity to performatively embody it (Alexander 2006: 549–53).[1] In this sense, Alexander perceives a great proximity between his analytical enterprise and, for example, the contemporary performance arts.[2] This position is in line with the developments of (cultural) sociology but also points towards an engagement with aesthetics in contemporary social life. Moreover, because it is directly implied in any activity of representation of the symbolic forms that engage any representation, aesthetics is also associated with power in two ways: it foregrounds the *power of representation* and the *representation of power*. These two sides of the problematic developed by cultural sociology obviously underlie what we have seen of the theory and the analysis of the civil sphere, but their presence is revealed even more strongly in works from the last decade or so, where Alexander tackles them head on. These recent works constitute important landmarks in understanding the general contribution that this socio-logical project, which is still developing, intends to make. Let us first address the question of the *representation of power* before moving on to examine the *power of representation*. We will then detail the elements contributing to a more general aesthetic of social life.

Empirical analysis of political life: the representation of power

In three successive books, Alexander devoted himself to an empirical analysis of American political life centered on the presidency of Barack Obama (Alexander 2010a, 2011a; Alexander and Jaworski 2014). This direct analytical foray into US politics took on a practical – and even partisan – twist in the way it was conducted: As part of his analysis of the 2008 presidential election that is the subject of first volume, Alexander went as an observer to a weekend training camp for Democratic Party volunteers doing campaign fieldwork in Denver (Alexander 2010a). Volunteers were trained to build a solid base from which the Obama campaign organization could engage voters at the polls, from direct (door-to-door) and telephone contacts to recreational events (dinners, barbecues, etc.) that carried messages of support for the Democratic candidacy and direct mobilization efforts for the election. Long months of preparation were required, including of course the initial recruitment of volunteers, but the main effort was the August 2008 volunteer training "camp" that Alexander attended, a gathering of 150 to 200 young people (mostly of Latin American origin) in a high-school amphitheater, where they were informed about the formulas and techniques of voter recruitment. On a national scale in the United States, tens of thousands of similar volunteers were recruited in order to ensure one of the two key elements of an electoral campaign: participation and money.[3] The training was provided by professional mobilizers (about twenty Democratic Party organizers, paid minimum wage) and an organizing expert responsible for teaching the volunteers the basics – but, crucially, in a way that emphasized the *personal relationship* between volunteers and the voters, not just recruiting them, but taking a genuine interest in their lives and their concerns (or at least appearing to do so).[4] This is especially necessary because in the US political system voters must register themselves to vote, so grassroots mobilization is critical and relies primarily on the ability to show that direct individual and collective involvement can make a real political difference at the polls by creating a sense of "community." In many states, minority voters (African-Americans, Latinos, etc.) were particularly targeted in this way, as their actual registration and turnout is often lower than average. The Democratic campaign relies heavily on grassroots mobilization to bring an often marginalized electorate to their side, possibly convincing voters to become members of the Democratic Party in the process, which greatly increases the likelihood of their vote. This is critical in the context of tight presidential election battles between Democrats and Republicans. By personally attending this weekend training camp, Alexander verified the atmosphere, techniques, strategies, and efforts involved, and, most importantly, the fact that they were counting on the mobilization of participation in order to make election activity more than just a media or publicity campaign. To be sure, the media effort was not absent (and in fact accounts for a substantial part of campaign expenses), but it often proves ineffective from the point of view of partisan gains, which can be better secured through "personalized" relationships. At the end of the weekend, volunteers were released to return to their hometowns scattered all over Colorado, where they also created other groups of volunteers themselves in order to maximize this electoral networking activity. Alexander's overall assessment, as well as that of many journalists and political analysts, is that this partisan networking activity enabled the Democratic Party to make the campaign – and Obama's victory – a major political event that allowed the symbolism of power to personally reach voters. It touched their hearts as this representation penetrated deep into civic engagement, personal emotion, social morality, and identification with a cause, leading to direct and effective involvement: voting and political participation (Alexander 2010a).

This example of mobilization reveals several issues, some of which have already emerged from the theorization of the civil sphere. We can see how collective representation can be created, requiring participant involvement that is moral in character, but also emotional – as we're still in the Durkheimian register of ritual – to which participants consent in the connection with something greater than themselves: the public fusion that generates collective enthusiasm in the realization of their individual reciprocal presence. Also present here is the idea that "carrier groups" (or *Gemeinde*, as Weber called them in his sociology of religion) are responsible for spreading and maintaining the message, and that effective individual mobilization is based on a commitment to political institutions. This corresponds to a certain vision of civil religion explicitly thematized in its American context by de Tocqueville in the nineteenth century, then revived in the 1980s through Bellah's religious sociology. But the forms of mobilization presented respond just as much to the requirements of the contemporary civil sphere, which must count on the capacity to "re-fuse" a society which – by definition since modernity – is fundamentally and increasingly "differentiated," or "de-fused." Indeed, this preoccupation lies at the heart of Alexander's project, in the political sphere of course, but more widely and deeply in any issue relating to the symbolic, as we will see below in connection to aesthetics.

Politics has its share of theatricality, which for Alexander is exactly where its symbolic hold is situated, and from which the representation of power draws its democratic foundation. An American presidential election campaign can be described, understood, and interpreted analytically according to its own drama, insofar as the elements of this theatricality are examined in terms of their overall participation in democratic institutional representation. The public, in this case the voters, can be reached directly through mobilization campaigns in the field and by organizers and volunteers who make sure that they participate effectively at the time of the vote, which shows how political representation is able to create adherence to the candidates' message. But other elements, such as the scenario, the "play" of the actors, the "staging" and their means (i.e. the different stages, public, media, etc.), should also be considered from the point of view of where (dramatic) ritual meets (political) strategy in terms of cultural pragmatics (Alexander and Mast 2006). In the 2008 campaign that first brought Obama to power, these elements were effective enough to produce a compelling and surprising, if not historic, political performance in terms of perhaps the most symbolically challenging element: the election of the first black president of the United States. But the Democratic campaign was able to count on a candidacy that defied stereotypes in this respect and that, above all, emphasized the charisma of its candidate in his eloquence and public performances, through which he managed to convey an image that went beyond the racism (subtle and explicit) that often taints American social and political life. In this respect, Obama even surpassed himself, in Alexander's eyes, in establishing a "heroic" figure against that of his Republican rival John McCain (himself an air force veteran and a "heroic" survivor of North Vietnamese prison camps). It should not be forgotten that among the president's main roles is commander-in-chief of the armed forces, and that this function of the executive branch always comes up as an issue in relation to the qualification of presidential candidacies – especially in contexts of high international tension, such as those related to terrorism since the beginning of the 2000s and the subsequent Iraq War.[5] All strategies – discursive, narrative, rhetorical, and staging – are deployed to make a candidate appear suitable for this position; in the case of Obama, an international tour of American bases and armed conflict zones in July 2008, skillfully planned to make it a real media campaign aimed precisely at this objective, probably helped achieve its goal of defeating McCain (Alexander 2010a: 155–8). This is obviously not the only way in which candidacies are prepared and staged, scrutinized as they are first by their campaign teams, then by the media, and finally by their political opponents. The personal, family, biographical, and professional strategies of each political clan are thus honed and adjusted according to the vagaries of political campaigns, but always according to a binary logic in which two options ultimately confront each other, because bipartisanship has remained the virtually unchanging rule in American politics since the founding of the two main parties in the nineteenth century.

This rule is itself, according to Alexander, related to the way in which the civil sphere is structured along the lines of the "structural hermeneutics" that fundamentally determine it. In the case of electoral campaigns, particularly presidential ones, it plays out in full by measuring itself directly against the candidates, according to their respective orientations and capacities to assert the values most likely to win favor with the electorate.[6] In two chapters examining these issues, Alexander shows how, beyond the "heroic" figure of the presidential candidate, "authenticity" must be demonstrated when dealing with political, social, and cultural issues. This includes the ability to situate oneself on a chessboard where delicate subjects abound, and where sincerity (beyond strategic calculation) and flexibility, as well as morality and reasonableness, of the future president must prevail.[7] This way of negotiating one's image appears to be decisive, caught between the various stratagems of the campaign teams, media responses, opinion polls, and real capacities of the candidates, who face pitfalls on a daily basis during the long months of the campaign until the fateful moment of the election. Questions surrounding fundamental orientations (civil or non-civil), politics (left or right), economics (liberal or conservative), religion (Christian or not), gender equality (progressive or retrograde), and "race" (inclusive/multiculturalist or exclusive/supremacist) all intervene at one time or another, finally making it possible to choose who will be carried to the pinnacle of power according to the most "just" representation that the electorate makes of it.[8] It goes without saying that the representation of power that Alexander invites us to accept has full credence in the process of representation as presented, without the cynicism and usual criticisms invoked to underline its defects and excesses. The "politics of the image," so decried in its American context since the 1960s, is not only endorsed in Alexander's work; it is even valorized, acquiring, as we shall see, a truly *iconic* dimension – that is, it underscores how symbolic representations come to establish an aura that is virtually "sacred" within the civil sphere. But because it is a somewhat manufactured representation, and thus artificial, part of the challenge is also to move beyond this artifice of representation towards "authenticity" and "sincerity." As Alexander writes:

To control the state in a democratic society means to become the chosen representative of the civil sphere. Normative theorists of democracy have understood this to mean that choice is a deliberative one. Social scientists have understood this choosing to be a reflection of social and economic conditions. In this essay, I advance an alternative view. To become a representative of the civil sphere is less a matter of rational deliberation than of symbolic representation. Politicians must become collective representations, textured and tactile images that inspire devotion, stimulate communication, and trigger interaction. This is hardly a matter of ritual, though the experience of highly affective scenes of fusion is ardently sought. It is a matter of controlling the image. It is to become a hero, to work the binaries while watching the boundaries. Pollution and purity are the aim, but partisanship must be avoided at all costs. Politics is performance, but political image cannot be seen as constructed. The media's new reflexivity is everywhere a danger. It threatens to undermine authenticity. Artificiality may be an attribution, but it often has the power to kill. (Alexander 2011a: 136)

This analytical position is the result not of naivety or ignorance of critical responses to the "politics of the image" but, on the contrary, of the will to subscribe fully to the symbolic structures in place within our societies. However, and as these are constituted by democratic principles where criticism truly has its place, one cannot simply overlook tendencies which not only intervene in the development of social and political life but even sometimes come to threaten the symbolic structures in place. While the importance of money has been criticized for the role it plays in politics, allowing for increased means of representation and wider access to channels of dissemination (essentially through advertising), in Alexander's view this does not contradict the fact that ultimately the symbolic expression of the political message remains decisive in the whole process (Alexander 2010a: 40–1). Another aspect of the way Alexander presents things could also raise certain questions about the extreme lability of the "icons" produced through the active manipulation of images, discourses, actions, strategies, and stagings. Indeed, this is one of the subjects of the book devoted to Obama's re-election, which notes how, in this context, we witnessed the "deflation" of the presidential symbol during the mid-term elections in 2010 (when the Republicans regained a majority in the House of Representatives and left a small Democratic majority in the Senate). This, however, poses a deeper question, which has crossed the horizon of mass democratic societies since the nineteenth century (Alexander and Jaworski 2014: 10–35),[9] and which de Tocqueville had already considered within what he called (well before Weber's polytheism of values) the "pantheism" of societies freed from religion as the official basis of their structures (Tocqueville 2004: 512–13).[10] The question of "civil religion," referenced by Alexander's concept of the "civil sphere," despite the much more political meaning he gives it, is intended to reinforce a political sphere left entirely free to choose its symbolic reference points by imposing a certain cultural tradition as the ballast for political practices. However, catastrophic examples, such as the fascist and Nazi movements, punctuate the history of the twentieth century to remind us that these features of mass democracies can lead to ideological excesses in which mythologizing simply becomes mystification – and one wonders to what extent the cultural sociology of the civil sphere can theorize such examples, based on a so-called formal grounding of the conditions associated with a healthy democratic life.[11] But another point must also be stressed, which has to do with the political dynamics itself created in this context of mass democracy: the diffusion of power through the body politic ensures not only that power and its legitimacy rest in the hands of the *demos* (understanding that one must then reach out to each individual to make sure that their vote is registered in the right place) but also that this situation, in which power makes sure that it is represented, rests fundamentally on the *power of representation.*

Power of representation: performance and dramatic action in the civil sphere

Cultural sociology relies on the autonomy of representations within the civil sphere – that is, on the precedence of symbolic representations over all other considerations in the capacity to define the exercise of power within society. So, from this point of view, where a definition of power prevails that is not only coercive but must rely on the performative, power must succeed in making sure that there is public adherence to its representation. As Alexander points out:

> In contemporary societies, audiences for political performances are often physically distant and emotionally disconnected, without affection or understanding for the mediated figures they see struggling for power. Citizen-audiences do not feel compelled to believe the truth of what they hear or see, much less to attribute to political performances emotional and moral force. While political performances must achieve success, contemporary audiences are increasingly de-fused from these powers that be. The struggle to re-fuse speaker and audience, to connect with the members of civil society through felicitous performance of the codes and narratives that define it – this is what the democratic struggle for democratic power is all about. (Alexander 2011a: 103)

The fact that symbolic representations achieve this effectiveness from the point of view of politics presents power as naturally being at stake in the context of a presidential election, where the representation of power becomes crucial. As we have seen, this is crucial even before the exercise of political power, when the capacity to exercise this power in the eyes of the electorate is determined by choosing a candidate for the presidential role. Fundamentally, however, the representation of power depends on the power of representation, a central theoretical innovation in Alexander's cultural sociology. In this perspective, power is not so much linked to the structures set up in our societies, in the exercise of domination, as to the capacity of symbolic representations to *express* political issues, according to the legitimacy that the power of representation grants them. This capacity is not limited to the exercise of power within the structures as such; it belongs to the symbolic representations themselves, all of which have the capacity to transform themselves into (political) power within the civil sphere. This is what Alexander presents, among other things, as the capacity of "counter-performance," or "contesting" the performance of power.[12] Here, one convincing example is that of the civil rights movement, which between the 1950s and 1960s exercised such a counter-power, in terms of the symbolic representations it developed, that was itself instituted as a power (Alexander 2011a: 147–58). In 1964 it was enshrined in law as the Civil Rights Act, which, by officially putting an end to racial discrimination in the United States, opened up an entirely new political scene. Other examples are also invoked, such as that of September 11, 2001, when terrorist "counter-performance" and counter-power struck at the very heart of prominent symbols of the "New World Order," targeting the twin towers of the World Trade Center in New York City, an event widely perceived not only politically but also aesthetically, a "performance" of an altogether different order. Alexander considers that terrorism, in general, by expressing and exercising violence within the civil sphere, belongs to a "post-political" register, where it is a question of acting through the horror and shock caused by a challenge to the very foundations of power (ibid.: 159–83). However, for Alexander, the symbolic expression of terrorism itself excludes on principle the establishment of a new political order because it is animated solely by a will to destruction. So the counter-performance becomes contrary to the one that could be anticipated. In the case of the September 11 attacks, it was a reaction to the power in place that consolidated its foundations – even if, of course, the direct effects of the "war on terrorism" that followed in Iraq and Afghanistan also provoked more or less convincing performances and counter-performances from a political point of view.[13] It is still the case, however, that, in all these circumstances, it is always the symbolic representation of each of these actions that is at stake and is staged – it is the power of representation to achieve its ends (or not) in the context of the civil sphere.[14] The power of representation thus maintains an ambivalent relation to the representation of power: any symbolic expression, from the point of view of its aesthetic performance, is a bearer of power, and even the political power in place must count on this capacity of aesthetic performance in the expression of its power. This culminates in the production of the "icons" of social life, which are those representations that come to possess a particular power of attraction within the civil sphere.

The power of the symbolic and the iconic

The interest in this symbolic category of icons designates a high point in Alexander's thinking: it allows for the articulation in a much more specific way of the relation between aesthetics and the power of representation. This is a junction that allows materiality to come into contact with the symbolic, justifying the definition of iconicity as the "interaction of surface and depth" (Alexander, Bartmański, and Giesen 2012: 2). All symbolic meanings find a material form which externalizes the internal resonance provoked by this in emotional, normative, and cognitive dimensions.[15] In the register of certain strains of semiotics (Peircian in particular), as well as in art history, the icon possesses a particular status because it is attached to the resemblance established by a specific symbolic domain: the sacred. Religious icons, which offer themselves as so many replicas of a symbol assumed by a relatively stable tradition, translate a symbolic order to which they refer. The meaning given to the icon in cultural sociology is significantly different from the derivative character attributed to it by Peirce, because it becomes *in itself* the presentation of the symbolic order that it embodies.[16] The icon is indeed more than the simple representation of the symbolic order; it actively *reproduces* this symbolic order. In a semiotic perspective that is close to Barthes's *Mythologies* (2013), Alexander insists on seeing the contemporary icon as a determinant of social, cultural, and artistic practices in general – including, of course, the political representations through which certain individuals (such as Barack Obama or Martin Luther King) become true *icons*.[17] It is not only "primitive" societies that, through totemism for example, have erected iconic symbols of their identity; modern and postmodern societies also possess their own institutional modality of such representations, which allow for a physical relationship to their own reality. From a perspective where anthropology rubs shoulders with psychoanalysis, the emotional attachment to iconicity translates a participation with the social order according to the prevailing codes.[18] Through iconicity, an "object's aesthetic power inserts the general into the specific, making the abstract concrete in a compelling and original way" (Alexander 2010b: 15), a capacity embodied in the artist, the designer, or any other person with the quality of *bricoleur* (in Lévi-Strauss's sense). This is particularly obvious in the case where iconicity is associated with celebrity, in a media world capable of promoting any object or individual, provided that their characteristics are likely to be specific attractors capable of producing modes of personal identification. These "models" that celebrities become thus possess, in Alexander's eyes, practically quasi-divine qualities, and to a certain extent this contradicts – through their exceptionality and relative permanence – the Warholian principle of "15 minutes of fame" extended to all (Alexander 2010c).[19]

The contribution of iconicity to cultural sociology is the identification of this relationship between the aesthetic dimension proper to icons in their material surface and the symbolic depth of a moral order within the civil sphere to which they are attached. The analytical task of showing this relationship is accomplished on the level of sociological theory, but is in fact just as much a matter of the capacity to "decipher" icons, in a world that has abandoned the fixed reference points of traditional religion, in order to establish its own reference points in a dynamic social evolution oriented by politics. Iconic power thus explicitly calls for the formulation of a "hermeneutic power" able not only to feel iconic qualities but also to translate them on the sociological level, because the performativity of icons is also linked to their diffusion in the public sphere, and in this way it is carried out according to their widened inter- pretation – which can be in the framework of specialized aesthetic criticism as much as of sociological analytics (Alexander 2012b, 2011c). Here, again, it is a question not only of "describing" but also of engaging in the promotion of symbolic expressions that possess a strong meaning and with a political propensity to participation in the civil sphere which must be underlined. And because it touches on society as a whole (as perceived according to its aesthetic charac- teristics) it is to the theatricality of social life that Alexander turns in order to illustrate in the broadest possible way the virtualities of a symbolic representation where aesthetics joins ethics.

A generalized social theatricality: the dramatic aesthetics of social action

The question of theatricality may appear to be an extension of the realm of performance – or, conversely, performance and performativity may appear as spatiotemporal reductions of theatricality, where it then becomes malleable and expandable almost *ad infinitum*. However, in the contemporary context where theater has become almost confused with performance (especially according to Richard Schechner (2003) and Victor Turner (1982), from whom Alexander borrows), the question has arisen about theater's capacity to adequately represent social life – that is to say, to correspond to the great issues that this life weaves and to bring them to light through a symbolic expression that is able to do them justice. In a context where twentieth-century avant-garde theater pursued experimentation of all kinds, pushing theatricality to the extreme limits of its capacity – towards complete disappearance in its most radical experiments, or becoming "post-dramatic" where the representation of social life is ignored completely – the situation can seem extremely complex and confusing (Alexander 2014a; see also Alexander 2017a). Alexander acknowledges this situation, exacerbated by the relative marginality into which theater has fallen since the advent of other media (such as film, television, and the internet) but reaffirms (following Raymond Williams) that theatricality is paradoxically more important today than ever. However, as Alexander also mentions: "[d]emocratic movements to control power cannot afford to be postdramatic," adding that "the invigorating experience of myth and value is the goal for which both aesthetic and social performances strive" (Alexander 2014a: 20). Thus, by rejecting a part of theatrical experimentation, that which does not produce a "re-fusion" of social experience, cultural sociology develops its own analytical perspective.

This reflection on the art of theater and social theatricality is based on a revision of the recent history of symbolic expression in the context of "de-fused" societies. Theater as such, in its Western origins among the ancient Greeks, already testifies to the distance of representation in relation to ritual, although Nietzsche understood the kinship that continues to exist on this level and inaugurated this "return to the source" of theatricality. This path was also followed by avant-garde experimentation as much as theory, and this inspired sociology, as Alexander located many fundamental symbolic reference points of a ritualistic order in contemporary theater. As mentioned, various theatrical experiments pushed representation to the extreme, from Brecht, who used a distancing effect which was able to make the audience become aware of the alienation of representation, to Antonin Artaud and Joseph Chaikin, who attempted to close this distance. For Alexander, Brecht and Artaud did not so much push theater beyond its limits as change the limits of what the symbolic expression of our world makes possible: either de-fusion or re-fusion. It is thus a question of drawing the lessons from these experiments, not so much to exploit them in themselves as to separate what is allowed to pass from the aesthetic sphere to the civil sphere, to "re-fuse" experience. Sociological analysis enables a link between the aesthetic dimension of theater and performance to the general theatricality of social life, especially from a moral point of view.

Cultural sociology thus helps reveal this social theatricality in action, through representations, by locating their anchor points at the level of their underlying moral codifications. This interpretation, which calls for a properly hermeneutic approach, is based on a reflexivity that adds to social theatrical performances the performativity of analysis itself. As Alexander specifies:

> The social power of intellectuals depends on their acquisition of performative power. Esoteric theories have to be simplified into action-centered scripts; action plans have to be drawn up, charismatic actors recruited, staff and followers organized and trained, detailed plans for reorganizing social life prepared, and powerful, publicly visible actions have to be put into the scene. Intellectual power is always performative, but the social power of ideas is another thing. It must be organized and displayed outside the academy, to audiences whose interests are less esoteric and more concerned with everyday life things. (Alexander 2017a: 8–9)

The task of sociological analysis is to achieve active participation in the development of a democratic, inclusive, egalitarian, and just social life. As such, the power of intellectuals working in the direction of cultural sociology must be powerful enough to "create symbolic frameworks that re-fuse fragmented meanings, actions and institutions" in order to "provide a new horizon of meaning for social actors who, having lost the sense of social and cultural circumstance, experience emotional anxiety and existential stress." In order to direct dramatic ideational power, "intellectuals must encode and narrate newly emerging social realities in a manner that offers salvation" (ibid.: 107). Without such a dramatization, "collective and personal meanings could not be sustained, evil could not be identified, and justice would be impossible to obtain" (ibid.: 141).[20]

The examples to which this theatricalization of social life applies are obviously multiple, and we have touched on some of them in the preceding chapters, but above all they are subject to becoming objects of "societalization" – a term Alexander uses to designate the process by which social questions come to be universalized within the civil sphere. Thus, elements of social life are identified, represented, and staged according to their capacity to embody moral outrage, then repaired by social and institutional processes – as shown by the "crises" that have erupted, for example, around issues of pedophilia within the Church, sexual harassment through the #MeToo movement, financial scandals, and other violations of moral codes (Alexander 2019). The task of analysis is to interpret through a description that can identify the (highly mediated) representations of these events, integrating them into a broader narrative that highlights their participation in the civil sphere as part of an evolving moral order, but according to a codification of democratic culture.[21] Again, the credence given to media representations (or those on social media) is not questioned but, rather, endorsed by cultural sociology from the point of view of the narrative that cultural sociology itself gives of various aspects of social life; relying on media representations helps furthering the social narratives into their *dramatic* content.

Cultural sociology is tuned into the media universe in order to draw from it a dramatization that is not only aesthetic but also moral in the sense of its connection to the codes of the civil sphere, and thus in solidarity with the journalistic experience – despite the profound transformations affecting this profession today, torn between technological innovations in the world of communication and information and economic problems due to the displacement of advertising revenue. Alexander has examined these issues and found that, in the end, personal convictions and professional organizations make it possible to consider that the union between journalism and democracy is always – and must remain – as intimate as possible, because their fundamental values converge in the structuring of the civil sphere (Alexander et al. 2016).[22] However, it follows that, even while it can borrow some journalistic conventions and representations, sociological analysis must push further in its "dramatization," using the symbolic structures relative to the underlying codification of social expression. In this respect, we can again point out that avant-garde theatrical experiments, by challenging the very structures of theatricality, have undoubtedly resulted in considerable transformations that cultural sociology could or should also take into account. The "scene of the body" in Artaud's theater of cruelty or the distancing of the "drama" in Brecht, to say nothing of Gertrude Stein's "stream of consciousness" theater, informed us of new forms of reflexivity that have emerged alongside developments in the contemporary media universe. These include new expressive forms linked to the embodied anchoring of performativity, the reversal of old narrations and stories of the contemporary world, and the decentering of individual subjectivity – all characteristics that have fundamentally restructured the experience of contemporary theatricality (Côté 2011, 2021).

Conclusion

At the end of the journey that has led us into the heart of the cultural sociology developed by Jeffrey C. Alexander, we can propose a brief assessment of his achievements, but we must also consider the present and future developments of this new analytical perspective within the sociological discipline. The project of cultural sociology is in full development, and particularly with regard to the concept of the civil sphere; indeed, analyses of cultural sociology will reach an international scale in this way.[1] In recent years, collective works have been published that follow the analytical perspective developed by Alexander in various national contexts, grouped in regional studies involving Latin America, Asia, the Nordic countries, Canada, and India.[2] The idea behind these works is not just to study the political dynamics emerging in societies around the world resulting from the expansion of mass democracies, but also to show the relevance of political dynamics from the angle of cultural sociology using the idea of the civil sphere. We can speak in this sense of an internationalization of analyses touching the civil sphere, or of the universalization of this concept resulting from Alexander's cultural sociology, which may enable the consolidation of a contemporary theory about the internal and external dynamics of our societies.

The project of cultural sociology has been pursued mainly by English-speaking sociology but today is increasingly adding international dimensions. This is allowing the sociological project to renew itself in its epistemological, theoretical, and analytical (or practical) resources, while ensuring an empirical foundation for its efforts to redefine sociology. In this sense, Alexander's sociological project is as much in line with the objectives of the "strong program" of cultural sociology that he set out to achieve some twenty years ago as it is with the objectives of rethinking classical and contemporary sociology in new ways and with renewed possibilities for development – this has been his purpose since the beginning some forty years ago. These two aspects of cultural sociology alone are rare enough within the discipline to be hailed as major achievements.

As we have also seen here, these developments and realizations raise issues for sociological analysis, presenting questions and problems that sociology must continue to explore. The fundamentally reflexive epistemological approach advanced – proposing not to ignore the scientific content of analyses but to go beyond the strict "objectivity" of the observations, propositions, and arguments put forward – finds its realization in a context where it can be criticized for a commitment to the very values that support the project of the civil sphere (democracy, inclusion, solidarity, and justice). It can just as well, on the other hand, call for a Gadamerian-style hermeneutic. Indeed, the "scientistic" attitude that justifies the search for simple objectivity today appears less pressing than an attitude that acknowledges scientific activity participating in the development of society. In this respect it is inevitably confronted with the double task of evaluating its own contribution to this development through its own practice, and also working (through pedagogy and other means) towards a reconciliation of scientific and social discourse. But this hermeneutical position, assumed by Alexander on the dual level of reinterpreting the sociological tradition and analyzing social life, also presents challenges that go to the heart of his analyses.

The first of these challenges is to draw from the sociological tradition a reading that can reveal its possibilities and limits – the scope of which we have seen in Alexander's work, which mainly engages with Marx, Durkheim, Weber and Parsons, as well as others such as Geertz, Bellah, Eisenstadt, and

Shechner. The reactualization of certain concepts inherited from classical sociology, extended in a critique that seeks to preserve their achievements while limiting their scope – often in relation to their socio-historical anchors and the contexts of their enunciation – allows for a renewal of this tradition without losing the threads of the fundamental questions that have woven the discipline. To make a new start in sociology does not mean ignoring the contributions that have allowed these questions to be brought to us, as if sociology had wandered aimlessly until now – as some of its current supporters suggest. On the contrary, it is always a question of understanding, explaining, and interpreting social life in the forms it adopts in the present course of its evolution, testing the answers brought by the sociological tradition and amending some of its developments – noting the richness of its contributions without pretending to start again from scratch with "models" cobbled together in a more or less original way. Of course, one can contest the interpretations that are then made of this sociological tradition in several ways: interrogating the relevance of a distinction between the sacred and profane within the civil sphere, for example; questioning the possibility of applying typical perspectives with regard to rationalization and modernity in the context of contemporary society; or returning to the meaning of a "societal community," whether national or international – but these are precisely the issues that still affect the present evolution of the sociological discipline itself.

The second of these challenges, obviously related to the first in its rearticulations of the sociological tradition being developed today, concerns the hermeneutics of social life proposed by Alexander's cultural sociology. With reference to the underlying codification of the civil sphere, and again in accordance with a Gadamerian perspective that endorses the idea of a "historically effected consciousness" within cultural traditions, we can stress that the contribution of cultural sociology, fertile as it is in its consideration of the deep symbolic structures of the social order, could, on the other hand, undoubtedly consider this dynamic more profitably using a dialectical method. If one perceives the international effervescence of the civil sphere as mobilizing underlying cultural codes, one must also count on the fact that these codes are also in transformation when put in contact with the contemporary realities of our societies. The universal extension of mass democracy, which seems to be a strong tendency in our time, pushed by international political relations where Western (European and North American) positions predominate, cannot occur without an intense dialogue with the strong symbolic structures that have determined cultures, sometimes for thousands of years (let us think of Indian, Asian, or pre-Columbian societies). To perceive the dialectical relationship that any society maintains with its culture, while accepting that it is indeed within a civil sphere that this relationship can be politically mediated, implies the recognition that cultural transformations take place in this way and that cultural codifications are themselves dragged into these transformations to be "recodified." This can be seen, for example, in the recodification of the symbolic structures of Western society, which since the nineteenth century have opened the door precisely to the development of mass democracies (which de Tocqueville was the first to observe in the American context). The autonomy granted to culture by cultural sociology implies that the symbolic forms and structures constituting culture are themselves the object of transformations. In other words, the irruption of the civil sphere as a point of reference for the transformations of contemporary societies on the international level must recognize that all the cultures and cultural traditions involved are directly implicated in the way these transformations are carried out. To speak of the revolutionary movement associated with the Arab Spring, for example, brings into play both the public manifestations associated with democratization and the mobilization of the cultural traditions then solicited – this can, to be sure, develop as much in a traditional direction as in a new and progressive one – as events from the past decade have shown.[3] The same might be said of the dynamics of political mobilization in Asian, Indian, European, South American, and North American contexts.

What we are witnessing in our contemporary societies, from the point of view of cultural sociology, is a vast global transformation giving rise to new ideas about the symbolic structures involved.[4] This movement is triggering a whole series of antagonisms revealing themselves within the civil

sphere, using the means and devices of theatricality in order
to establish a universalist recognition of the principles of
political participation in mass democracy. This aesthetic
dimension of social life is linked to social movements seeking
social justice, and so the main analytic strand within the civil
sphere presents itself as a search for normative mechanisms
aimed at repairing injustices. For cultural sociology, however,
it is not so much a question of aiming for a perfect theoretical
model capable of defining norms in an abstract way, as Jürgen
Habermas does, as one of following the indications provided
by the dynamics offered by socio-political actors, as well as
media representations of these actors, in order to reconstruct
a "dramatic history" of the social and cultural transformations in progress. In the same way, the analyses one can
draw from such situations do not lead to a final statement
because they rest on the contingency of these manifestations,
and thus on judgments that are contextual, contingent, and
never definitive. The proposed interpretations of social life
are globally perceived from the theoretical point of view of
the civil sphere as being carried by the *hope* that this allows
us to glimpse – that of a democratic, inclusive, solidary,
and just society – and cultural sociology positions itself as
a contributor to this project because it understands its own
reflexive position.[5]

Alexander's cultural sociology has inspired, and continues
to support, the development of a renewed perspective among
many contemporary sociologists because it allows for the
continued possibility of reflecting on the major social issues
of our era while at the same time promoting a renewal of
the sociological discipline. In this sense, the achievements
of cultural sociology testify to the vitality of an analytical
perspective which, far from solving all the problems it faces,
at least allows us to pursue and deepen the dialogue – and the
dialectic – between sociology and society.

Notes

Introduction

1 The present book, in its French version, filled an important gap in francophone sociology that ignores almost completely both cultural sociology and Alexander's work, with the notable exception of Vandenberghe (2000), and also Cefaï (2007: 467–545), who devotes a long chapter to developments in cultural sociology while noting Alexander's contribution. I believe that even more fertile connections are possible between the work of Cefaï and Quéré, especially on the question of public space and social theatricality – see Côté (2021). When the British journal *Cultural Sociology* was launched, the first editorial made it clear that Alexander's cultural sociology was already making its mark in the discipline, while they also opened the door to contributions that would more broadly embrace "sociology of culture" in their orientation (Inglis et al. 2007).

Chapter 1   The "Strong Program" of Cultural Sociology

1 For Bloor (1991: 7–8), these are the principles of causality (relative to the social conditions that determine beliefs and knowledge), impartiality (relative to the truth or falsity, the rationality or irrationality of beliefs and knowledge), and symmetry (relative to the explanation of the causes). See also Barnes (1974). Bloor's reliance on Durkheim's *The Elementary Forms of Religious Life* (especially the last part, which links totemic categorizations to the origin of scientific knowledge)

as the basis for his own sociology of knowledge enterprise was certainly important for what would become Alexander's project, despite the criticism of "sociological materialism" that he ascribed to Bloor (Alexander 1982a: 116–67). We shall return to this question in chapter 2.

2 Thus they do not take into account, for example, Raymond Williams's distinction between dominant, emergent, and residual cultures, nor do they provide an alternative to the analysis of power presented by *Cultural Studies*, Bourdieu, and Foucault. It is in the thread of the subsequent argument that these questions will be restated here in a fresh way from the point of view of cultural sociology, particularly with respect to Alexander.

3 The expression "cultural sociology" is in fact used for the first time, but without being clearly defined, in the first volume of Alexander's *Theoretical Logic in Sociology: Positivism, Presuppositions, and Current Controversies* (1982a: 125) in direct connection with the analyses of Clifford Geertz, who was later identified by Alexander as one of the main inspirations of cultural sociology when it became the official designation of a project to reform the sociological discipline.

4 I will alternate between these designations of "human" and "cultural" sciences to refer to what is also called "social sciences." All three terms are distinct from the natural sciences, but to speak of "social sciences" would be to some extent to short-circuit the integration of the resources of literary theory or semiotics, or of philosophy and other disciplines, whereas the aim is to remain as open as possible on this level while broadly favoring references to the domain of culture.

5 I am using here a vocabulary that Alexander does not use; there is no question for him, at this moment, of "symbolic structures" or of "objectification relation" to designate the subject–object relation present in the definition of scientific activity. It is for the sake of clarity, where a terminology that includes the "symbols" and "structures" of social and cultural life will intervene in the analysis of signification, that I opt for this vocabulary from now on.

6 In fact, Alexander proposes a scale that allows us to distinguish the elements that make up the scientific process; these range from the presuppositions that point to the properly metaphysical environment of science to the observational statements that point to the physical environment. Between these are other levels – starting from the metaphysical environment of presuppositions there are: ideological orientations, scientific models, concepts, definitions, classifications, laws, simple and

complex propositions, and methodological principles. This
tiering is presented in a horizontal form and thus does not
presume the precedence of the metaphysical dimension over
the physical dimension, or the reverse; instead, it relies on
the ineradicable link between the two, according to the steps
involved in the theoretical logic.

7 There would be much more to say about the "hesitations"
of sociology between Kantianism or neo-Kantianism, in
their categorical distinction between sciences of nature and
sciences of culture (as in Weber, Rickert, Windelband, etc.), and
Hegelian philosophy, which unites these two enterprises within
logic (or the science of logic). Dilthey (2010) speaks rather of
Geisteswissenschaften (sciences of the mind) to designate the
same disciplines. Habermas ([1968] 1987) does not resolve
this hesitation by distinguishing three distinct "orders" of
knowledge (which in Hegelian philosophy would in fact appear
only as three "moments" of the same logical process), whereas
Alexander, wanting to preserve the logical unity of theorization,
does not distinguish between these three moments – which
can be problematic with respect to the "critical" moment in
particular, because the dialectic can be short-circuited at this
moment, as we shall see in particular in chapter 3.

8 I underline here in passing that this problem is already present
in the first use of the term "ideology," by Destutt de Tracy
(1970) at the very beginning of the nineteenth century. Tracy
considered it to be "science of the idea," and it was the basis of
his system of knowledge (this is a remarkable proximity – even
if it is only apparent – with Hegelian philosophy, which ignores
the term "ideology" in order to be concerned only with the
"science of the Idea"). The essentially *political* sense that the
term "ideology" acquired should be placed within the history
of ideas of the nineteenth century, which goes from Napoleon
(designating de Tracy and his other political opponents as
"ideologists") to Marx (criticizing the "German ideology" as
much in philosophy as in politics), which did nothing to help
clarify the ambiguity of the term.

9 The coincidence of the rise of Parsonian theory with the first
reforms that would lead to the advent of the welfare state in the
United States during Roosevelt's New Deal in the 1930s, as well
as the consolidation of both approaches in the post-World War
II era, has been well analyzed by Buxton (1985).

10 I give here only a very general overview of the many authors
who are examined and criticized by Alexander in chapter 3
(1982a: 64–112). Any reader interested in the details of these

criticisms, which are precise, extremely varied, and concern a large number of authors (many of whom are not always well known today) should refer directly to this chapter.

11 These major developments in Parsonian sociology are introduced later than the synthesis presented in *The Structure of Social Action* of 1937, in *The Social System* of 1951.

12 In Europe, Parsons's influence has been felt mainly in Germany (Niklas Luhmann, Jürgen Habermas), England (Anthony Giddens), Italy (Ino Rossi, Giuseppe Sciortino), and, to a lesser extent, France (François Bourricaud, François Chazel, Alain Touraine). Parsons was also introduced in Quebec sociology by Guy Rocher.

13 The AGIL system constitutes in fact the fundamental original formalization of all Parsons's theorization of action stemming from the sociological synthesis that he proposes.

14 The terms "maintenance" and "survival" appear to be interchangeable because, for Parsons, the fundamental reference model remains biological; it is by differentiation from its environment, and the establishment of relations with it, that an organism comes into existence, and this requires on its part a capacity for *adaptation*, for the pursuit of *goals* (feeding, reproduction, etc.), for the *integration of* external conditions into its own interior through different functions, and then for *latency* with respect to the different external and internal stimuli, in order for its existence to be maintained. When one of these elements fails the organism is in danger, and its disappearance is in fact only its definitive integration into its environment (i.e. its non-differentiation from it, as in death). This "bio-logical" foundation of the Parsonian theory (one might also say its onto-epistemological reference), which he drew from his physiologicalist colleague Lawrence J. Henderson at Harvard in the 1930s, would not be contested by Alexander, which is surprising because it contradicts on the epistemological level the distinction between the natural sciences and the cultural sciences. Alexander does not ignore this crucial filiation of Talcott Parsons from Henderson, but neither does he point out the epistemological (and even onto-epistemological) contradiction (Alexander 1985a: 8). The same might be said of Luhmanian systematization, which will further reinforce (however possible that be) this association of sociology with biology.

15 In the introduction to his edited book *Neofunctionalism*, Alexander summarizes these positions as follows: "Within a neo-functionalist framework, materialist reference is never

separated from culture or personality systems; contingency is related to systemic process; ideological criticism of society occurs within a multifaced understanding of social differentiation; and thinking about conflict is intertwined with theories of integration and societal solidarity" (Alexander 1985a: 16).

16 It is in his book *Neofunctionalism and After* (1998b) that this break with neofunctionalism was announced, retrospectively, and that the new orientation of cultural sociology was simultaneously announced, in connection with the problematic of the *civil sphere*.

17 If one were to continue the parallel with William Buxton's (1985) analysis of Parsons, one might consider the societal context of the emergence of Alexander's theorizing with the rise of neoliberalism in the 1980s when state integration was under attack – this would allow for, among other things, the rise of "civil society" in social and sociological concerns. The theory that Alexander later developed in his book *The Civil Sphere* (2006) clearly shows this orientation, as we will see in chapter 4.

18 We shall return at the end of this chapter and in chapter 6 to the crucial distinction between "actors," "agents," "individuals," and "persons" that is involved in Alexander's views.

19 One can get a good idea of the intense and feverish activities of the Center for Cultural Sociology at Yale University by visiting its website: https://ccs.yale.edu. It was Alexander's arrival at Yale in 2001 (he had previously been a professor for twenty-five years at the University of California, Los Angeles (UCLA), hosting the "Culture Club" among other things in the 1980s and 1990s) that prompted the establishment of the CCS in 2002, along with his colleagues Philip Smith and Ron Eyerman.

20 The expression "church" might make us smile because of its ambiguity, especially since cultural sociology is making a return to what will be called Durkheim's "religious sociology"; coupled with the injunction to produce a reflexive analysis, this return could almost be seen as a way of "sacralizing" cultural practices – a tension that will not always be absent from certain analyses, and which would be a real contradiction in terms for sociology as a scientific discipline. The fact, however, that cultural sociology assumes its scientific character by opening up to the debates that it itself entails (rather than closing itself up to a dogmatic approach) appears salutary in this context (Alexander, Jacobs, and Smith 2012: 11).

21 Turner (1985) reviews the first volume of *Theoretical Logic in Sociology, Positivism, Presuppositions, and Current*

Controversies, and offers a devastating – but in my view not entirely justified – critique of Alexander's approach, pointing out the vagueness of his argument and suggesting it is unfounded. The rest of Alexander's analytical project, in its coherence and systematicity, seems to me to prove Turner's criticism wrong.

22 See in particular Kurasawa (2004) and Roberge (2009), both of whom point to this difficulty in seeing how Alexander's approach allows us to go beyond (in its criticisms of) critical theory, or simply social criticism – we will return to this question in chapter 3 in particular. McLennan (2005) has also criticized the development of cultural sociology for its idealist and, in places, simplistic and naive bias. We will return to these criticisms as well in our own terms, but for now we will limit our references to these commentators on Alexander's work, who are too numerous to be taken into account in a systematic way.

23 To the influences of Bellah and Geertz, one should add Smelser, Eisenstadt, and also Edward A. Tiryakian, whose brief commentary on the 1979 eulogy offered to Parsons, emphasizing the continuation of structural functionalism in terms of attention to the religious and affective, is retained by Alexander (1983b: 482–3, n. 55).

24 If one still perceives Parsons's influence in the coupling of the terms "action" and "order," and even in subjective will, which Parsons considered to be a determinate of American culture (under the name of "individual activism" – on this subject see Parsons (2007)). We can also see that Alexander goes even further in terms of the latitude given to the expressive possibilities of cultural symbols.

25 See the chapter on Geertz's works, both apologetic and critical: "Cultural Sociology (2): Clifford Geertz's Rebellion against Determinism," in Alexander (1987: 303–29). The use of the expression "cultural sociology" in this book is still close to the expression "Cultural Studies" used until the mid-1990s, while Alexander's critique of Geertz will also open the way for his own conception of the *civil sphere* as the typical principle of a dynamic social order open to its transformations, which will have to be sociologically analyzed by hermeneutics.

26 It is precisely this "formal" character of the philosophy of symbolic forms that Cassirer has often been reproached for, and rightly so, since, by preventing himself from recognizing a hierarchy and a pre-eminence of certain symbolic forms (at least until his very last works), he jeopardized his capacity to discriminate certain contemporary issues. This criticism of

Cassirer, formulated as much in the hermeneutics of Hans-Georg Gadamer as in that of Paul Ricœur, however, hinders the recognition of the properly historical (and sociological) task of managing to distinguish different horizons of meaning to be attributed as much to historical as to "epistemic" regimes.

27 The *rational* character of law for Hegel (i.e. the fact that it is the product of human Reason) does not mean that it does not nevertheless undergo the test of its *finite* conditions of existence in the expression of the modern state – and that it is therefore eventually overtaken, in Hegel's own formulation, by the consequences of historical development. This is what Marx, first, and then Weber and others, on so many different levels, will come to notice – and this opens the fundamental problem of sociology, which is to manage to recapture society in its self-constituted forms, recognized as properly human (and no longer divine).

28 De Tocqueville thus opened a path that was to be followed by Robert N. Bellah (Bellah et al. 1985) and subsequently Alexander.

29 A fundamental issue appears here that is worth noting: in the *Elements of the Philosophy of Right*, Hegel could afford to consider that the activity of establishing the rational framework of law (and, in the first place, its fundamental anchoring in the constitution as the "law of laws") of states was established on the strict basis of its (textual) expression by human Reason. Now, the whole of the subsequent evolution of modern bourgeois democracy has consisted in the transformation of these laws (and even of constitutional laws), which has brought legislative activity to the forefront, especially for a sociology eager to identify not only social transformations but societal evolution itself. In relation to Hegel, some proponents of pragmatism (especially John Dewey and George Herbert Mead) have focused their analytical and theoretical efforts on capturing this political dynamic – thanks to the political reformism inherent in the mass democracies they embraced. Thus, for example, Mead theorized that it was the political capacity for societal transformation, implied in the recognition of a constitutional possibility of self-transformation that characterizes contemporary society – on this see Côté (2015: 58–63).

30 Unfortunately for us, Mauss ends his exercise, as we know, at the end of the eighteenth century and the beginning of the nineteenth century (Kant and Fichte) – that is to say, at the very moment when philosophy, in particular, starts a fundamental re-examination of this question – which we can follow in part in George Herbert Mead's *Movements of Thought in the*

Nineteenth Century (1936: 85–152), as well as, of course, in the theorization of the "self" in Mead's *Mind, Self, and Society* (1934).

Chapter 2 A Rereading of Durkheim

1 For both Marx and Durkheim, Alexander distinguishes between early work and late work, and it is the early Marx that will interest him more, whereas, for Durkheim, it is the late work. In this volume, the title of which makes the point clear, Alexander will try to put the two authors back to back, on the basis of Marx's materialism and Durkheim's idealism, in order to take advantage of this opposition by rejecting some of their positions while preserving some of their achievements – we will come back in more detail to what Alexander retains from Marx (and above all, what he rejects from him) in the next chapter. Indeed, Alexander considers – and this is the reason why he deals with both authors at the same time – that the tension between collective determinism and voluntary individualism finds its climax in this encounter: the emphasis the later Marx puts on structures prevents him from considering individual possibilities, while the later Durkheim, by relying on voluntary action in collective movements, weakens the presence of structures. Thus, for Alexander, "the dialectic between Durkheim and Marx illuminates the central dilemmas of sociology" (1982b: 80).

2 The title of the book immediately indicates the ambivalence that still marks the not yet fully defined orientation of a true cultural sociology; English Cultural Studies, inherited from Birmingham, had by then spread to the United States and taken an important place in sociological analysis. It is in this context, as we shall see in the next chapter, that the project of cultural sociology will definitely develop and take a firmer configuration.

3 Indeed, the opposition between "sacred" and "profane" will evolve towards a semiotic opposition between "good" and "bad," or even "positive" and "negative," which diminishes the charge of, let's say, "religion" that it could have included at the beginning – and this is done by means of an evolution of religion towards the consideration of a *civil religion*, first, and then towards the "civil sphere," in the course of the development of a reflection which will also assume the greatest part of Weber's historical sociology, concerned with the transformations affecting the passage from a "sociology of religion" to a "sociology of culture" (of which cultural sociology will want to take note) while incorporating a contemporary reflection

on "performance" as distinct from "ritual." The reading of
Durkheim, whose legacy in Mauss had perhaps accentuated the
philosophical anthropology in certain works, will then find a
reorientation. See Alexander and Smith in their introduction,
entitled "The New Durkheim," to their edited work *The
Cambridge Companion to Durkheim* (2005: 1–37).

4 In this short note, Alexander criticizes Hans-Georg Gadamer,
Charles Taylor, and Richard Bernstein for adopting a hermeneutical program that is only "formal" – again a terse criticism,
which perhaps needs to be tempered, if not completely revised,
when one is ready to tackle the philosophical issues involved.

5 Alexander is obviously not the first commentator to have
emphasized this reorientation of Durkheim's sociological
project in a "second phase" stemming from his encounter
with the religious phenomenon, and one can even say that he
follows Talcott Parsons quite closely in this, as Pizarro-Noël
(2014) points out. The differences with respect to Parsons are,
however, quite significant and do not, in my view, lead to the
full convergence with Alexander that Pizarro-Noël maintains,
because the "voluntarism" implied in this reading of Durkheim
also includes, for Alexander, the recognition of the collective
character of representations.

6 Alexander relies on the reading of late texts (i.e. after 1893–4)
and posthumous works such as *Moral Education* and *Sociology
and Philosophy*, where Durkheim develops these ideas. The
interest of this rereading will also be reflected in chapter 4,
where we shall see Alexander's critical rereading of Weber's
sociology of religion. Alexander will underline the aporia that
Weber created by making Protestantism the ultimate religious
form of the modern world, being simultaneously unable to give
meaning and significance to modernity – other than through
its reduction to strict instrumental rationality. This is a fundamental question in the meaning that Alexander attributes
to contemporary society in his reading of it; this is why I
distinguish "sacred," with quotation marks, in the context of
Alexander's cultural sociology.

7 Alexander draws the notions of "pollution" and "purification"
from the work of the British anthropologist Mary Douglas,
who herself developed her perspective based on the notion of
"taboo," "extending Durkheim's original understanding ...,
demonstrating that every symbolization of sacred purity is
classified according to an impure element to which is attributed
a power of pollution" (Alexander 1988b: 217).

8 This analysis marks the first step of Alexander's entry into

the analysis of political things from the angle of morality; it will continue thereafter by being refined through the use of the theory of "performance," as we shall see later, in chapters 5 and 6. This orientation originated at the very beginning of Alexander's work, as we have already pointed out in noting the "double hermeneutic" required in his theoretical logic, and it accompanies him throughout the development of his thought, in his very precise hermeneutic sense. See, among others, Alexander (2000).

9 Although the reference to structuralism is linked to Saussurean *semiology*, I prefer to use the term "semiotics" here, which refers to another tradition of thought (initiated by Charles Sanders Peirce, a founding figure of American pragmatism), since it is ultimately to this tradition that Alexander will end up linking his analytical project – while at the same time retaining a terminology that differs from it, especially in relation to iconicity. Other considerations, such as the categorizations established by Peirce, which are hardly conceivable in the *semiological* tradition (from Lévi-Strauss to Barthes, who are also significant for Alexander), will become apparent later on to motivate this terminological choice.

10 This definition of the dialectical virtuality of symbolic forms, based on their fundamental definition, is found in Cassirer (2000).

11 These different aspects of the follow-up to the Watergate analysis would be enough to feed a voluminous study, which of course goes far beyond our present concerns. They are nevertheless important to keep in mind, since they bear witness not only to real political life in the United States but also to the transformations of American politics over time. They are, in other words, "reconstructions" that affect the meaning and significance of political practices, regardless of whether they are "sacred" or "profane." Alexander is not deaf to the demands for transformations of symbolic expressions, but, by presenting them in the form of "codifications" that are introduced through social discourses, he insists on locating "a continuity in the deep structure from which these discourses are derived and to which they must appeal" (Alexander and Smith 1993, repr. in Alexander 2003: 141), in a way that remains up to a certain point static.

12 An example, taken from Cassirer's philosophy of symbolic forms (1944), allows us to grasp what it is all about: for Cassirer, if the myth possesses an "expressive" function above all, we must also count on "representative" and "significant"

functions, which are expressed respectively in the registers of language and science. This implies, of course, the recognition of symbolic forms according to the function they occupy in the social and historical world. This formalization of the symbolic, in the register of the functions that it assumes, can seem unduly linked to the neo-Kantianism associated with Cassirer, but it becomes meaningful when applied to the reading of contemporary phenomena such as Nazism; the essentially "mythical" form of its ideological expression does not correspond to the requirements of the political or the function of scientific expression in this domain (Cassirer 1946).

13 This rereading is important in more than one respect, since it will open not only to the perception of the transformations of the signification operated in contexts of symbolic action but also to transformations of the cultural order – according to the principles raised in the previous chapter (we will come back to it more in detail in chapter 4) – and that by opening the analysis of cultural sociology to the performative dimension of social life.

14 Gianni Vattimo writes on this subject:

> But this problem is precisely that of secularization; it is a problem that cannot be solved by pretending to read the biblical texts above all as *texts* – texts which, like the other great messages of the past, belong to or, rather, constitute the tradition to which we belong. The biblical texts claim a specific *normativity*, and it is precisely around this normativity that, in our culture, the very concept of text is constituted and articulated (it would not be difficult to show that text is originally a concept heavy with normative pretensions; the text on which a society and a culture take their model is above all a text; even today, in everyday language, the text is above all the "book of the text," the text that, in a certain way, "makes text"). There is no theory of interpretation and textuality, perhaps not even semiotics, without a thematization of secularization. (Vattimo 1991: 62–3, my translation; emphasis in original)

15 References by Alexander to Victor Turner and Clifford Geertz are already present in various places in the four volumes of *Theoretical Logic in Sociology*, but they will become more assertive and deeper with *Durkheimian Sociology: Cultural Studies* (1988a).

Chapter 3 A Critique of Marx, Cultural Studies, and Bourdieu

1 Alexander offers his reading of Marx in the second volume of *Theoretical Logic in Sociology* (1982b) in an alternation with

his reading of Durkheim. This volume presents, in a singular way, chapters devoted to the first writings of Marx, to the first writings of Durkheim, and then to the late writings of each of them; finally, it devotes chapters to the continuations of Marx in Marxism and to the continuations of Durkheim in "Durkheimism." The presentation that I give here thus seems to separate what is, on the contrary, a true cross-reading of these two authors. I believe, however, that this method is justified by working through a coherent and, let us say, more "didactic" development of Alexander's sociological thought.

2 This place left open for theology is not negligible, since, on the one hand, it touches on the impossibility of the knowledge of the "thing-in-itself" and, on the other, it assigns to the possible experience of any knowledge, in its transcendental aesthetics, the external limits that are for this experience the time and the space, which are *a priori* conditions of the experience that knowledge can never reach either, because it depends on them for its own constitution. These two categories are thus left in indeterminacy (or infinity) – and beyond theology they thus open the door to utopia.

3 I recall that Hegel's major work, the *Encyclopedia of the Philosophical Sciences*, is composed of these three parts: *Science of Logic*, *Philosophy of Nature*, and *Philosophy of Mind*. The systematic character of the whole is revealed according to a dialectical logic where each category proceeds from its opposition to its "other" (or its negative), then to an overcoming of this opposition in a third term. Thus: "being" is opposed to "non-being," and the term which exceeds this opposition (by including the two antecedent terms) is "becoming." This development of categories, which is not only "structural" but also "dialectical," culminates in the third figure of the absolute Mind, which is science (or philosophy – an equivalent term in Hegel's case), whose requirement is to give a full account of its object – which comes back to the source or departure of the exposition of logic, thus completing the systematic (some critics say circular) character of the exposition.

4 Hegel's philosophy opposed religion, by showing the "finite" character of the various religions (in his *Lectures on the Philosophy of Religion*), while at the same time situating Christianity as a crowning achievement, and by assuming it entirely within his own philosophy (in a reflexive moment of "surpassing" its theological content, which has become a historical revelation of its historical effectivity). The consequences of this development exceed of course the framework of

our present work, but they can nevertheless be seen in the developments offered by hermeneutics – notably by Paul Ricœur.

5 The ever stronger affirmation of the autonomy of culture also serves as a basis for the intended distinction from the "sociology of culture" (Alexander 1996a), as discussed in chapter 1.

6 I purposely use Raymond Williams's categories of "dominant," "residual," and "emergent" cultures, associating them with social strata, in order to facilitate understanding. In Williams's case, this categorization is not so rigid (since "residual" culture may well, among other things, be associated with atavistic elements of popular culture, for example, and is not restricted to aristocratic culture).

7 See Stuart Hall's classic, perhaps even canonical, text, originally published in 1973, "Encoding and Decoding in the Television Discourse" (Hall 2021). I do not insist here on the internal debates of this development, which, for example, opposed the more orthodox Marxism of Raymond Williams to the "semiotic Marxism" of Stuart Hall, except to underline that the developments of English Cultural Studies have been precisely inhabited by internal tensions. There are nevertheless other possible connections to be made between *Cultural Studies* and cultural sociology, notably in the use that both approaches make of "rituals" – despite their different perspectives.

8 See "The British Are Coming ... Again! The Hidden Agenda of 'Cultural Studies'?" (Sherwood et al. 1993). This article is in fact a book review essay of Grossberg, Nelson, and Treicher's *Cultural Studies* (1991). In their rather acerbic review of this book, which was intended to anchor the English *Cultural Studies* movement in the United States, Alexander and his colleagues point out that the studies on culture developed by various authors (Geertz, Turner, Bellah, etc.) have nothing to learn from this Marxist-inspired approach – or from analyses that simply confuse culture and power. The summary description that I give of Cultural Studies, by linking them to Raymond Williams and Richard Hoggart, aims only at contextualizing this approach, by referring to authors that Alexander unfortunately does not examine in his critique of Marxism summarized above.

9 The whole question of subjective reflexivity, which serves as a counterweight to cultural sociology, comes from Alexander's analysis of Weberian sociology, as well as from the "phenomenological" approach stemming from pragmatism and its aftermath (in symbolic interactionism and ethnomethodology), as we shall see in the next chapter.

10 This critique is developed in a long chapter in Alexander's *Fin*

de siècle Social Theory: Relativism, Reduction, and the Problem of Reason (1995: 128–212). We will have the opportunity to come back to this work because the issue it presents – that is to say, the question of Reason in its contemporary context – is central to the whole discussion on modernity and its aftermath, with which Alexander cannot avoid engaging – particularly in his critique of Weber.

11 Although when Alexander's collaboration with Michèle Lamont was established it reduced their theoretical and analytical differences. See, among others, Lamont and Fournier (1992), which contains a contribution by Alexander. In the review of Alexander's book which critiques Bourdieu, Lamont partially endorses his critique, relying, however, on the possibilities of rereading Bourdieu more fruitfully (Lamont 1998).

12 Alexander points out in this respect that individual subjectivity is defined in such a way as to deprive it of any possibility of autonomy. He refers to George Herbert Mead's concept of 'Self' (Alexander 1995: 137); he also points out that the individual is not the only thing to be defined in this way – he could as well show that, according to Mead, it is the concept of habit which is questioned in the ontogeny of the consciousness of oneself ("self-consciousness"), and thus this concept of habit, although it can be brought closer to the concept of *habitus* for Bourdieu, is necessarily and profoundly different from it, because it is directly involved in the changes that take place in the social order, since becoming reflexively aware of habits is the first step to take in order to try to transform them – on this subject, I refer again to my work, *George Herbert Mead's Concept of Society: A Critical Reconstruction* (Côté 2015). The difference in political philosophy, which for Mead's pragmatism is rooted in social reformism, appears to be antithetical to Bourdieu's when placed on this level.

13 I make this remark, of course, as a reminder of Bourdieu's critique of Heidegger's "political ontology" (Bourdieu 1988). The reversal of such a reflection vis-à-vis Bourdieu's positions reveals that his fundamental model remains that of "the struggle of all against all." This is, among other things, what Alexander will criticize, at the end of his book, showing that a political vision that goes beyond utilitarianism is absent from Bourdieu's work, and that it must, on the contrary, constitute the normative center of cultural sociology.

14 Among other critics of this reductionist perspective, Alexander cites, for example, Caillé (1981).

15 There is much to say here about Habermas's project of renewing

critical theory within the Frankfurt School, since, in what can be called a major turn towards a theory of communication (as opposed to the earlier Frankfurt project of a critique of Reason), Habermas was to break with his illustrious predecessors. Informed by the studies carried out in the framework of *The Structural Transformation of the Public Sphere*, which emphasized the legitimacy of political deliberation offered by bourgeois democracies for enlightenment and emancipation through the public use of reason, Habermas subsequently integrated some of the principles of American pragmatism (from Charles Sanders Peirce and John Dewey to George Herbert Mead) in the 1960s and 1970s, and then of Parsonian sociology, in the pursuit of what would become his "theory of communicative action" in the early 1980s. It is this movement that brings him singularly close to Alexander's enterprise, in the latter's project of going beyond Parsons by rereading the sociological tradition. The fact that Alexander's efforts will culminate in a cultural sociology prioritizing the "civil sphere," where analyses of symbolic expressions prevail, brings him singularly close to Habermas, except that Habermas's theoretical enterprise cannot correspond to what Alexander sees as a sociological project going beyond the "critical" (and let's say "utopian") horizon of the theory of "communicative action."

Chapter 4   Culture, Politics, and Civil Religion

1 We recall that, in the case of Durkheim and Marx, Alexander tried to detect in the "early writings" the lineaments of the presuppositions that fed the future developments of their sociological analyses, while at the same time pointing out the contradictions that arose in the works in relation to their initial intentions. This is more difficult with Weber, in Alexander's eyes, because of the caesura that intervenes in the development of his thought, and whose first writings attached to economic history contrast with the efforts of sociological formalization that intervene thereafter. Nevertheless, we can see Alexander's hermeneutical concern to link the works of these authors to their biographical anchors in order, if not to "understand the author better than he understood himself," according to Schleiermacher's principle taken up by Dilthey, at least to relativize the positions developed in favor of their insertion in a very precise socio-historical context surrounding their individual experiences.

2 As it goes, "sociology of culture" designates then here as much what Weber and Simmel called "sciences of culture"

(*Kulturwissenschaften*) as what Dilthey called on his side the "sciences of the mind" (*Geisteswissenschaften*), based on his approach uniting both Schleiermacher's hermeneutics and Hegel's philosophy. Together with Cassirer's own contribution to the *Kulturwissenschaften*, these provide the closest allies of Alexander's own cultural sociology.

3 The exception being here the question of "reason" within Western society, which makes the specificity of this "historical individuality," as Weber likes to situate his analysis of civilizations (which then present themselves as generalities) while preserving the orientation of the sciences of culture (focused on particularity). It is then the destiny of this Western rationality, animated by a finality, if not a teleology (justifying its transhistorical maintenance, always present in the enterprise of sociology itself as a science), that becomes the problem tapping the Weberian enterprise. Alexander does not quite put things on the background of this properly epistemological tension but, nevertheless, situates it on other levels (notably methodological and ideological).

4 Here, it is Weber's attachment to the principles of neo-Kantianism (and the maintenance of a different logic applied to the sciences of nature and the sciences of culture which prevents the latter from really developing "concepts," having to be satisfied with presenting "ideal types" of a hypothetical character), on the one hand, and his lack of theorization of what really constitutes a symbolic form, on the other, which prevent him, at least it seems to me, from succeeding in proposing an adequate solution to the problem of the analysis of signification. Stripped of their inherent dialectical character (as Cassirer (2000) will apprehend it, for example, in the continuations of the project of the sciences of the culture), the "symbolic forms" simply assimilated to the "meanings" are thus classified according to idealistic categories which rigidify unnecessarily their plasticity. Alexander for his part will only criticize the analytical side of Weber's position – rather than his theoretical position – by showing that he is being reductionist by privileging the definition of "instrumental action" (*Zweckrationalität*) as the central motive of the development of modernity.

5 The text is titled "The Cultural Grounds of Rationalization: Sect and Democracy versus the Iron Cage," and appears as chapter 3 of Alexander's *Structure and Meaning: Rethinking Classical Sociology* (1989: 101–22), but it was the subject of an earlier, much shorter version, co-authored with Colin Loader, which appeared in the journal *Sociological Theory* (Loader and

Alexander 1985). Weber's text "Churches and Sects in North America" was first published in English translation in 1985 and may have motivated Loader and Alexander's article – though Alexander already refers to the German version in his book on Weber (Alexander 1983a: 99) but without giving it the significance, crucial in my view for his own analytical enterprise, that he would later attribute to it.

6 Weber's sharp analytical eye, based essentially on his personal observations, had already been the subject of similar reflection within the framework of Protestant morality in the United States of the eighteenth century; in the context of the first and second "Great Awakening" movements, where Protestant authorities were concerned that the social – or even popular – character of these events, carried by stars of public preaching such as Jonathan Edwards, largely took precedence over the religious or theological content they were supposed to represent. On this subject, see the works of Perry Miller (in particular *Errand into the Wilderness*, 1964: 153–66).

7 I would like to point out that this distinction, which has become classic in sociology, between "community" and "society," established by Tönnies, was to be reiterated by Talcott Parsons in the combined form of the "*societal community*," in particular in his later writings on the characterization of American society (see in particular Talcott Parsons's *The System of Modern Societies* (1971) as well as his posthumous work *American Society: A Theory of the Societal Community* published in 2007 at the initiative of the Italian sociologist Giuseppe Sciortino, who wrote the introduction, and in which Alexander signed a short foreword). This notion of "societal community" will in turn eventually be used by Alexander, as we shall see in chapter 5.

8 I also refer here, beyond the criticisms of the reduction of the meaning of charisma historically in Alexander's work on Weber cited here, to the chapter entitled "The Dialectic of Individuation and Domination: Weber's Rationalization Theory and Beyond" (Alexander 1989: 68–99), where he cites a number of authors, sociologists (Durkheim, Parsons, Habermas), economists (such as Keynes) and other thinkers (such as Piaget) who, in his view, participate in a different analysis of modernity, one that is likely to lead to more positive judgments about it than those maintained by Weber. We will of course come back to this question shortly. Another way of looking at the reversals taking place within the social transformations themselves, in the religious and economic domains, would be, for example,

to consider seriously the passage from Protestant asceticism to consumerist hedonism at the turn of the nineteenth and twentieth centuries, as Daniel Bell does in his book *The Cultural Contradictions of Capitalism* (1976).

9 However, we can underline here that it is precisely in this sense that Weber could be criticized by the proponents of contemporary hermeneutics, in particular Paul Ricœur; just as Ricœur reproached Freud for his one-sided interpretation of religion (Ricœur 1965: 407–528), Weber could be criticized for having proceeded, in his examination of "Protestant morality," to an excessive formalization which, by artificially extracting elements from certain theological texts, allows itself to recompose them in a relatively arbitrary "synoptic table" (ideal typification) which becomes their substitute. If Ricœur derives his critique of Freud from a hermeneutical argument (that the interpretation of texts derives its value from its capacity to interpret their overall meaning, and not only from a part), one could just as well see in it an epistemological critique of the ideal type, a procedure by which Weber's sociology intends to treat all social and historical phenomena but which fails precisely because of the same defect of "arbitrary" reconstruction of the meaning it intends to tackle. We can consider that this distance between Weber and hermeneutics is already present in the difference that is established with the work of Dilthey, from the beginning of the twentieth century, in the quarrels of "methods" (*Methodenstreit*) that were then raging in Germany.

10 In the immediate aftermath of the statement of principle aimed at the "meaning of social activity" – that is to say, the meaning given by actors to their activity, in relation to the means used and the ends aimed at, in particular with regard to others – Weber enumerates three major classes of meaning: subjective, the average within a group, and the "pure type" constructed as a "type" by the actors. It seems that the rest of his sociology was preoccupied above all with this last category of meanings, which fits well with his own methodology of the ideal type – but which rigidifies and distorts the forms given to meaning by reducing them to the arbitrariness of his own analytical construction. Alfred Schütz will try to take back this Weberian perspective with a little more flexibility by reformulating in more varied "typifications" the formalizations introduced by Weber. Alexander does not, however, pay sustained attention to it when he approaches this contemporary side of phenomenology.

11 This direct filiation with Mead claimed by Blumer has been the subject of numerous challenges since the 1970s (and even

a little earlier, by, among others, Anselm Strauss (1956), in a different version he gives of symbolic interactionism). The abusive reduction that Blumer made in his reading of Mead, under the cover of a naturalistic scientism, seems in fact to have constituted the passing of an important heritage of sociology, while at the same time having constituted a kind of obstacle to a richer reading of Mead to be inscribed in sociology – something which the revival of "Meadian studies," initiated by Hans Joas (1985), has partly remedied. Nor should we fail to point out that everything that is considered to have come out of the Chicago School in sociology (Robert E. Park, William I. Thomas, Florian Znaniecki, etc.), being affiliated in a more or less faithful way with pragmatism, could just as well be found in this framework – but Alexander does not pay attention to them.

12 Alexander seems to be unaware, in this respect, that Goffman joins Durkheim in an even more profound way when he points out that it is because the "person" has become a societal and cultural symbolic category that it comes to be the object of such rituals and reverences in the social activities of representation (including self-representation) – see on this subject Erving Goffman, *The Presentation of Self in Everyday Life* (1959). This is particularly important for the continuation of cultural sociology, when it will itself stage the dramaturgical analysis of social life on different bases, and we will thus come back to it while dealing with this question; what will then differentiate cultural sociology from Goffmanian sociology will be the accentuation of the strategic (one might even say "rhetorical") character of representations.

13 By pointing to the "indexicality" of practices (i.e. their relation to a particular empirical situation), Garfinkel opts for a category derived from Charles Sanders Peirce's semiotics, which definitely brings him closer to pragmatism – well beyond what he himself is ready to acknowledge. This filiation is most of the time ignored by ethnomethodologists, cutting them off from the other semiotic categories (such as icons and symbols) that are also included in Peirce's semiotics.

14 Alexander argues that this turning point in Garfinkel's analysis (he was also a colleague in the sociology department at UCLA) comes with the publication of Garfinkel's now classic book *Studies in Ethnomethodology* (1967).

15 I say approaches stemming from pragmatism, and not pragmatist approaches, because for a few decades a rediscovery of pragmatism has been taking place beyond what had been

known from these approaches that we have mentioned previously. Alexander himself is sensitive to this distance between pragmatism and the so-called strictly interactionist approaches, mentioning that George Herbert Mead reveals more than has been retained by Blumer and others (Alexander 1987: 195–214, 290).

16 We recall that these two approaches emerged from the debates within neo-Kantianism in Germany at the turn of the nineteenth and twentieth centuries. Dilthey is certainly the one who, while maintaining a certain allegiance to neo-Kantianism by the distinction he makes between natural sciences and "sciences of the mind," makes the greatest rapprochement with Hegelianism – noticeable not only in his work on Hegel but in his use of a terminology that is close to it, in his implicit links with the *Philosophy of Mind* (the third part of the *Encyclopedia of Philosophical Sciences*).

17 As we have seen above, it can also be said that hermeneutics has been part of Alexander's preoccupations since the very beginning of his theorizing enterprise. However, although the inflection given to this perspective in the sense of a "structural hermeneutics" suits the program of cultural sociology by allowing him to refer to a cultural tradition erected in more or less permanent symbolic codes, it raises certain questions about its capacity to welcome interpretations of a more dialectical character insisting on the transformations which are emerging on the level of the socio-historical evolution of societies. This is a wide and deep question because of its epistemological, theoretical and methodological resonances, which requires in my opinion a separate treatment.

18 To which it should be added that, as discussed in chapter 1, Bellah accompanied Alexander on his doctoral journey at UCLA before they became colleagues in the Department of Sociology there. Upon Bellah's death in 2013, Alexander wrote in a short eulogy that "the cultural sociological community lost its last living founder" (Alexander 2014b), noting how a work such as *Habits of the Heart* (Bellah et al. 1985, to which one might also add Bellah et al., *The Good Society*, 1992) had marked the kind of analyses pursued by cultural sociology.

19 It must be emphasized that modern bourgeois society, and the rise of the type of democracy it established through parliamentarianism and then revolutions (English, French, American, etc.), retained until the turn of the eighteenth and nineteenth centuries a strong foundation in religion (Christian, of course, both in Catholicism and Protestantism), from which it even

drew its ontological guarantees of theological character. It is only later, with the gradual advent of mass democracies in the nineteenth and twentieth centuries, that this foundation and these guarantees were diluted.

20 This theme, which Weber forges by rubbing shoulders with nineteenth-century concerns about polytheism, possibly following the abandonment of the cardinal reference to Christian monotheism (which interests John Stuart Mill as much as de Tocqueville, or even Hegel, who incidentally criticizes it), obviously takes on a particular importance in the context of the relativism that tends to spread within mass democracies – becoming a strong theme in postmodernity. Alexander wants to prevent this by always privileging a form of universalism, linked to civil religion, which will become for him the "civil sphere."

21 Thus, for him, civil society

> means trust in the universalistic values that abstract from any particular society and that provide critical leverage against particular historical actors. It guarantees the existence of a public, not public consensus or consent. Because of their trust in a higher universal order, citizens continually make demands to authorities to justify their actions. The higher order embodies ideal justice; because earthly authorities must inevitably violate this ideal norm, moral outrage is a continual result. In strong civil societies then, distrust of authoritative action and political conflict are omnipresent. Yet it is this very separation from endorsement of particular arrangements that makes democracy possible. Because the ultimate loyalty of citizens is to overarching rules rather than to the outcome of any particular game, policies and office holders can be changed, though the process may be difficult and subject to continual contestation. (Alexander 1991a: 169)

In the theorization of democracy that he puts forward in these terms, Alexander claims, among other things, a reading of Claude Lefort.

22 To clear up any ambiguity on this point, Alexander writes:

> I am not suggesting here that the national community should be understood simply as civil society, any more than it should be understood as a capitalist society, a nation-state, or a cultural community. Civil society must be understood analytically, not concretely. It is not a sphere that one can touch and see, any more than is the sphere of political power, economic production, or cultural life. It is a dimension that is organized by the fact that it subjects those who are its members to specific kinds of obligations and acts, which can be distinguished from, and are often in

conflict with, those of economic, political, and cultural ideology. The analytical nature of this sphere means that civil society can be understood as interpenetrating with, or permeating, these other spheres, just as the pressures of the latter are often interjected into public life. (Alexander 1991a: 168)

23 This program, based on the concept of the "civil sphere," was developed in the 1990s in the reflections on civil society and then launched in a more systematic way in Alexander's *The Civil Sphere* (2006). It is this analytical program that will give meaning to international analyses of the civil sphere a decade later.

24 The title of the article – "The Discourse of American Civil Society: A New Proposal for Cultural Studies" – makes it clear that "cultural sociology" had not yet quite emerged, at that time, as the original analytical program that would be thematized a few years later, also by Alexander and Smith, as we saw in chapter 1.

25 See in particular his short article "Sociological Theory and the Claim to Reason: Why the End Is Not in Sight" (1991b: 147), where Alexander writes, among other things: "To make a claim to reason ... is to suggest that sociological theory can achieve a perspective on society which is more extensive and more general than the theorist's particular lifeworld and the particular perspective of his or her social group." Alexander's inspiration from the hermeneutics of Dilthey and Gadamer, as well as his critique of relativism, is elaborately expressed in his text "General Theory in the Postpositivist Mode: The 'Epistemological Dilemma' and the Search for Present Reason," where he insists that "reason that is exercised vis-à-vis tradition in everyday life is exercised by the interpreter of society as well. Universalism and objectivity are intrinsic to the exercise of the modern human sciences; they mark its coming of age. ... Interpretive understanding is not simply personal and empathic; it necessarily involves an impersonal reference that allows a critical and universalist response" (Alexander 1992b: 355).

26 See, in particular, "Between Progress and Apocalypse: Social Theory and the Dream of Reason in the Twentieth Century," in Alexander, *Fin de siècle Social Theory* (1995: 65–89).

Chapter 5　The Civil Sphere and the "Societal Community"

1 Beyond those just named, we might add others such as Paul Colomy, Steven Seidman, Bernhard Giesen, Jason Mast, and Isaac Ariail Reed, as well as, of course, Philip Smith, his Yale

University colleague (and valued collaborator for more than twenty-five years), all of whom have at one time or another worked very closely with Alexander and contributed to the works that were developed at the Center for Cultural Sociology at Yale University.

2 In fact, the notion of "societal community" developed by Parsons (especially in his posthumous work, *American Society: A Theory of the Societal Community*, 2007), aiming at going beyond Tönnies's opposition community/society by merging the rules of law with the collective sense of morals, describes the "national solidarity" that is expressed through *citizenship* in Western societies, this political citizenship that has developed in a form of universalism according to a socio-historical process that culminates in the achievements of the contemporary world (Alexander 1983b: 96–9). Alexander's concept of the civil sphere will take up elements of this civic solidarity by voluntarily and explicitly going beyond Parsons's vision of the "societal community" (see Alexander's retrospective explanation, "Contradictions in the Societal Community: The Promise and Disappointment of Parsons's Concept" (2005a: 95)), but also extending it to a national *and* international context and subscribing to its greater "autonomy."

3 One of the clearest expressions of this position of the humanities remains that set out in Hans-Georg Gadamer's *Truth and Method* (1989).

4 Following the programmatic article published in 1993 with Philip Smith (Alexander and Smith 1993), Alexander focused on coupling the analysis of civil society, a "cultural sociology," with the conceptualization of the "civil sphere" as a critique of Parsons and to form a new theoretical synthesis. The various stages of this evolution can be traced in the following books and articles, among others: Alexander (1998a, 1998b, 2000, 2001). This sequence culminates in his 2006 book *The Civil Sphere*.

5 As he did for Marx, Durkheim, and Weber, Alexander examines the development of Parsons's thought in a rigorous way, noting that the three different periods (early, middle, and late) converge, in Parsons's case, without a break – except in the accentuation of certain features which will determine its ever narrower orientation (this is the case notably for the addition of cybernetics in the middle period). The question of the autonomy of culture, the Achilles heel of Parsonian sociology, is examined in particular in Alexander (1990).

6 As we have seen in the preceding chapters, it is by partly

redoing, and in a critical way, the path taken by Parsons (in particular in his first important work, *The Structure of Social Action*) that Alexander proposes a reading which, among other things, retains from Durkheim a greater attention to a social order welded together by the ritual performances associated with religion, and from Weber an accentuation of the importance given to the multidimensionality of sociological analysis. The passage through Marx and the abandonment of Pareto (contrary to what Parsons had done) also underline the specificity of Alexander's reading of classical sociology: leaving aside Marshall's marginalist economic views that Parsons integrated into his own synthesis, and replacing it with Marx, helped Alexander to perceive the conflictual dimension of social life, which he situates at the political level (instead of relying on the Marxian's insistence on economic structures).

7 Basically, the question at stake is that of the symbolic formation of meanings, which Parsons had seen in an ultimately cybernetic (and static) way, and which cultural sociology wants to see in a dynamic way.

8 On this personal experience of the 1960s, years of student unrest and protest, see Alexander (2005b).

9 It is this synthesis that opens up the program of cultural sociology in its analytical orientation towards what would become the theorization of the civil sphere. Reflecting on these ideas of Parsons, Alexander writes that he wanted to come up with "something beyond reconstructing the terms of Parsons' societal community" and what that entailed: "We need a new theory, one that recognizes, from the beginning, the tension between integration and justice. Separating the ideals of community from their uneven institutionalization, acknowledging that the symbolisations of collective identity depend on negative and not only positive symbols, such a new theory would begin from a recognition that exclusion and inclusion are dialectically related real existing societal communities" (Alexander 2005a: 98).

10 We can also see very well here how the theorization and the analysis that follows from it distances itself from the theory of *public sphere* in Jürgen Habermas: by avoiding the construction of a utopian and normative model of "unconstrained communication" within "communicative action," a path that according to Habermas allows the preservation of the achievements of modernity and the Enlightenment by combining them with the demands of the critique of the contemporary world (which has itself moved away from these ideals), Alexander dives instead

directly, analytically speaking, into the symbolic expressions that are formed in the context of participation in the civil sphere in order to draw lessons about how the dynamics of political transformations operate on the social and historical level. This analysis is then not so much critical of these developments as seeking to accompany them, in a reformist political sense, by bringing out their democratic, participatory, and inclusive dimensions within the civil sphere itself, which thus becomes their receptacle – while becoming the theoretical framework for analyzing them.

11 To the historical extension given here of the symbolic structure of civil society, Alexander is prepared to give an anthropological extension as well, pointing out how the ideal of the "democratic community" (with its qualities of inclusion, solidarity, and social justice) appears constitutive of all human societies. He writes:

> While this [democratic] community seems like an ideally Kantian one, it has been powerfully constructed only in very specific historical places and times. In broad brush terms, of course, the ideal of an enlarged community has been an imminent part of all human societies, from aboriginal bands to ancient civilizational empires like the Chinese, where conceptions of moral but especially ethical civility were widely accepted and in important respects remain so even today. Nonetheless, in its radically universalistic rather than primordial form, its emphasis on equality and its insistence on the autonomy of the individual, this conception can be traced back to more specific Western sources: to the transcendent community of ancient Israel and its extension to the "universal otherhood" of Christianity; to the Greek polis; to the communal movements and individualistic philosophies of the Renaissance; to the radical Puritan ideal of the community of all believers; to the Philosophes and the French revolutionary articulation of liberté/égalité/fraternité; to the ideals and practice of socialism in its Western form. (Alexander 2000b: 295–6)

12 Alexander devotes a chapter to each of these bodies, detailing their functions and roles in the overall dynamics of the civil sphere. I think it is important to emphasize that, in so doing, he introduces substantial modifications to the classical conception of civil society as found, for example, in Hegel's *Philosophy of Right*; thus, the representative functions of election, which in Hegel are part of the state sphere (and part of what he considers *ethical life* (or *Sittlichkeit*) – distinct from but inclusive of both legality and morality), are here placed directly in the civil sphere,

which certainly diminishes the distinction between them, but which in turn corresponds quite well to the development of the "social" as it has intruded between the "private" and the "public" since the advent of mass democracies. This way of conceptualizing the civil sphere also opposes Habermas's views about the fate of bourgeois civil society and the possibility of its reconstruction within a theory of "communicative action," as discussed at the end of chapter 3, as well as in note 11 above, especially since the civil sphere is capable of accommodating any expression within it (and not just the utopian ideal of "unconstrained communication").

13 As we will also see, this orientation is established in parallel with others, such as those of criticism (from Luc Boltanski and Laurent Thévenot in the horizon of justification, or from Axel Honneth in the horizon of recognition) – see, among others, Alexander (2015).

14 Alexander was at the Centre d'étude des mouvements sociaux at the École des hautes études en sciences sociales in Paris during a sabbatical in 1993–4. It is worth noting here, I think, that Touraine's distance from the "old social movements" (i.e. those more directly related to labor movements and associated with the Marxist movement until the 1960s) signals a closer proximity to the aims of cultural sociology – see, among other things, Alexander's review of Touraine's 1997 book *Pourrons-nous vivre ensemble?* (Alexander 1999). For his more general position on Touraine, see Alexander (1996b).

15 Touraine's *Critique de la modernité* (1992) and *Qu'est-ce que la démocratie?* (1994) are referred to by Alexander to provide the background for the evolution of his thinking as presented in the review of Touraine's book *Pourrons-nous vivre ensemble?* (Alexander 1999: 100, 104–5).

16 Here is a key passage on this:

> The alternative to state control via force is legitimate power, which occurs when obedience is voluntary rather than coerced, when rightness is attributed to power for moral reasons rather than for reasons of habituation or fear. This opportunity for will formation, to use Habermas' term, can be provided only when a "civil" realm exists that to some degree is separated not only from the state but also from the other "non-civil" spheres of religion, science, economy, family, and primordial communities. Such an independent civil sphere can exist only insofar as the privacy of individual interaction is protected, institutional independence is guaranteed for the creation of law and public opinion, and normative symbolic models make honesty, rationality, individual autonomy, cooperation, and impersonal trust

the basic criteria for membership in the binding community that defines "society." (Alexander 1996b: 225)

17 I speak here of a "dialectic," whereas, from Alexander's point of view, it is a transformation of the signifiers with respect to the signifieds, as we have seen in the quotation, which ensures that the fundamental "codes" of the civil sphere finally remain unchanged – ultimately restoring the terms of a "structural hermeneutics." I am for my part more inclined to consider that the codes change through these very movements, which instead indicates a "dialectical hermeneutics," likely to show the historical ruptures that occur, as well as the sutures with respect to these ruptures introduced by new symbolic mediations.

18 Although this social movement is fundamentally oriented by the African-American community, it includes others, and this was from the beginning in the claims made by the National Association for the Advancement of Colored People, from its foundation in 1909, which also included Hispanics and other visible minorities, and up to the Civil Rights Act of 1964, which excludes any form of discrimination based on "race" – that is, ethnicity or skin color – or religion.

19 These infamous laws to prevent newly freed slaves from voting or participating fully in society, passed by some of the Southern states that were resistant to equality following the abolition of slavery, were known to advocate the doctrine of "separate but equal" marked by racial segregation, which would last for almost a hundred years. This is what the civil rights movement attacked.

20 It should be noted here that, in Alexander's view, these more extreme expressions of the African-American community, which are also expressed in the separatist movements that set an exclusive agenda for the community (ranging from curriculum reforms to a return to the roots of Africanness), are seen as crossing the boundaries of the civil sphere.

21 This will be presented in terms of the "societalization of social problems," according to the title of Alexander's recent book *What Makes a Social Crisis? The Societalization of Social Problems* (2019). We shall see later on what this consists of more precisely, with the example of the Holocaust in particular, and then with other issues that have touched the news. However, we can immediately see in what the reference to Hegel implies, as much a shift of emphasis, which calls not for the observation of the completed realization of the universal (as the modern bourgeois state did in Hegelian philosophy) but, rather, for the project of its eventual realization or actualization

in the dynamics of a civil sphere that reaches international proportions.

22 Victor Turner and Richard Schechner (and particularly the latter, who will further accentuate the conclusions of the former of an aesthetic and dramatic vision of social life in the interpretation of the symbolic dimension of action) are often perceived, with good reason, as being at the heart of the development of the whole field of *performance studies*, which takes off from the end of the 1970s and the 1980s, and to which Alexander will pay specific attention from the beginning of the 2000s. This recourse to anthropology and theater thus becomes an important complement to the analyses of Geertz's symbolic anthropology and Bellah's sociology of religion (or those of civil religion), as seen in the previous chapter.

23 This application of thermodynamics to the cybernetic and animal worlds (moving the field of physics into the realm of information and biology), and then into the social world (into sociology), is what seems to me to reinforce the "naturalistic" content of Parsonian systemism – but it is not from this point of view that Alexander will develop his critique of Parsons, as mentioned in chapter 1.

24 We thus move from a reference to Saussure's linguistics (and to his famous explanation of the relationship between signifier and signified, which posits the only relative and negative value of the elements of meaning in relation to each other – on the phonetic as well as the semantic and semiotic level) to the linguistics of Roman Jakobson, in particular. It remains interesting to underline, in this respect, how Jakobson himself deals with the relationship between linguistics and cybernetics in the understanding of codification when he writes:

> The code matches the *signans* with its *signatum* and the *signatum* with its *signans*. Today, with respect to the treatment of coding problems in communication theory, the Saussurian dichotomy *langue/parole* can be restated much more precisely and acquires a new operational value. Conversely, in modern linguistics communication theory may find illuminating information about the stratified structure of the intricate language code in its various aspects. Although the framework of the language code has been adequately outlined in linguistics, it is still frequently overlooked that the finite ensemble of "standard representations" is limited to lexical symbols, their grammatical and phonological constituents, and the grammatical and phonological rules of combination. Only this portion of communication can be defined as a mere "activity of replicating representations." On the other hand, it is still opportune to recall that the code is not confined

to what communication engineers call "the bare intelligence content of the speech," but likewise the stylistic stratification of the lexical symbols and the allegedly "free" variation, both in their constitution and their combination rules, are "foreseen and provided for" by the code. (Jakobson 2010: 573)

25 Alexander makes this idea explicit in opposition to Parsons's more abstract classification:

It is not only the transcendental and free nature that creates new tensions, however, but the binary nature of symbolic classification itself. Universalism is not a choice that can exclude particularism from social life; it is a codified definition of categories of motives, relations, and institutions that derive their meaning only in relation to what is conceived as their opposites, that is, in relation to the categories of "excluded" and "particularist." The sacralized symbolic categories that constitute universalism, in other words, can only be defined by contrasting them publicly with the profane motives, relations and institutions that characterize other kinds of individuals, institutions and groups. It is for this reason that the excluded "other" always stands alongside those who are included in the civil sphere. An educationally generated reflexivity can never stand entirely outside these arbitrary elements of understanding; they are inherent in the process of meaning formation itself. (Alexander 1998b : 226–7)

26 See in this respect the different schematizations of this process by Alexander (2004a), where he presents the different phases of the process of representation of political performance. I refer the reader to these schematizations for a detailed explanation of the elements they contain, limiting myself here to pointing out the general lines of the process of performances stemming from cultural pragmatics in its relations to the civil sphere, as we will come back to it in the next chapter.

27 Alexander puts it this way: "In psychological terms, the relation between actor and text depends on cathexis. The relation between actor and audience, in turn, depends on the ability to project these emotions and textual patterns as moral evaluations" (2004a: 531).

28 The chapter entitled "Holocaust and Trauma: Restriction in Israel," on this duality of meaning of the Holocaust in the conflict between Israel and Palestine, is co-authored with Shai Dromi (Alexander 2012a: 97–117).

29 See particularly Alexander (2011b), Alexander and Tognato (2018), Alexander, Palmer et al. (2019), Alexander, Lund, and Voyer (2019), Alexander et al. (2021). Several other volumes

are in preparation in this series on the analysis of the civil sphere in the international context; these collective works, which have emerged from collaborations with many colleagues from different contexts, illustrate the development and scope of civil sphere theory as a potentially universal analytical framework and are, in sum, a demonstration of the breadth and validity of cultural sociology analytics today.

Chapter 6   The Power of Representation and the Representation of Power

1 By presenting his conclusion as a participation in the *project* of the civil sphere, Alexander thus shows both the theoretical and somewhat "civic" contribution of sociology in this context. It should be understood here that the analytical or theorizing activity of sociology is not in itself part of the civil sphere; like other categories of activity (related to family, work, religion, etc.), sociology has its own rules of operation and deployment. However, like other activities, it also has an impact on the civil sphere, and it is this impact that we are concerned with here, especially when it touches so closely, through analysis, on political issues. Its participation in the civil sphere is apparent in the debates in which cultural sociology may participate, examining the causes and effects of political phenomena, while not losing sight of the fact that this approach then enters the arena of the public sphere – which justifies not only its analytical enterprise but even its partisanship, which in Alexander is strongly inherited from the protest movements of the 1960s, as previously mentioned in connection with his biographical article "The Sixties and Me: From Cultural Revolution to Cultural Theory" (Alexander 2005b), in which is revealed, among other things, the place he reserves for the civil rights movement.

2 See, among others, his interview with Rodrigo Cordero, Francisco Carballo and José Ossandón (2008).

3 In Obama's 2012 re-election campaign, for which figures from the Democratic Party organization are given, these still speak for themselves: 2.2 million volunteers, active from 813 campaign offices, would have resulted in over 125 million "human contacts" (Alexander and Jaworski 2014: 101–2).

4 It is difficult to avoid thinking here of the analyses developed by Erving Goffman, who insists on the "staging" required in social situations where the aim is to persuade an audience of the truth of what is presented to them; indeed, in these voter recruitment campaigns, the aim is to obtain their support and their vote,

and thus the creation of "personal relationships" on which the trainers insist but which appears to be a relatively artificial motive. Alexander, who is familiar with Goffman's sociology and refers to it, does not, however, emphasize this aspect on this occasion.

5 This "heroic" image of the presidency in the United States has historical roots, particularly in the person of George Washington, the first president of the new republic and a "hero" of the Revolutionary War; it has been reflected in presidential figures who have also combined military "heroism" (such as Andrew Jackson, Ulysses S. Grant, or Dwight Eisenhower). Alexander addressed this aspect of the issue in a short article: "Heroes, Presidents, and Politics" (Alexander 2010c).

6 That this rule of bipartisanship is consistent with the "structural hermeneutics" of the civil sphere does not mean, of course, that the classification of oppositions corresponds point for point to either of the political parties involved. Historically, both parties, Democrats and Republicans, have contributed in their own way to strengthening one aspect or another of the civil sphere – but Alexander's view tends to favor the Democratic Party's orientation, particularly because of its positions on the civil rights struggle of the 1960s.

7 These remarks had value, one might say, *before* the election of Donald Trump, who appeared to change the rules of how politics works in the United States, but whose presidential term has since systematically put him in opposition to the institutions in place – witness the impeachment proceedings against him in December 2019 and again in December 2020. This "threat to institutions" has been examined by Alexander in two articles, on attacks on civil solidarity and Steven Bannon's ideology respectively (Alexander 2018a, 2017b).

8 In concluding their book on Obama's second-term victory in 2012, Alexander and Jaworski write:

> It is the performance of politics that determines the fate of political campaigns. Who can grasp the nettle of the collective consciousness? Who can write scripts fitting the great themes of national history to the particular challenges of this time and place? Who can persuade citizens that their election will bring national salvation, or at least prevent a terrible fall from grace? Who can become a compelling symbol of democratic hopes and dreams, sculpting a political image that embodies freedom and solidarity in a wise and worldly way? Whoever makes meaning better will be the winner in a presidential campaign. (2014: 108–9)

While it can be pointed out that the United States is undoubtedly a case in point with regard to its own image of its society (often seen as a global model), it is easy to see that this mechanics of the "providential" image is often invoked in other national contexts as well, when important policy choices about the overall direction of society are called into question.

9 The "deflation" experienced by the Obama symbol is attributable as much to the difficult social and economic conditions faced by the president in the early months of his first term as it is to the fact that he had in some ways retreated from the public sphere to focus on his presidential work – a diagnosis shared by Obama himself, as well as by many political commentators, and by Alexander and Jaworski. Changes in these two registers then contributed to a certain "re-inflation" of the Obama symbol during the 2012 re-election campaign.

10 If it seems that the context of Romanticism in which de Tocqueville writes is conducive to this adherence to pantheism, the properly political factors to which he attributes it continue to exert their force – if this logic of channeling individual interests for general, but also ephemeral, explanations to the changing conditions of societies continues.

11 Even taking into account the exceptional character of such movements on the historical level, associated with particular conjunctures and with the awful excesses to which they led (as the organization and the realization of the Holocaust attest), it is still the case that the techniques of mobilization at work in Nazism, for example, which had so much recourse to the aesthetic dimension of political activity, reveal an instructive part of present interests on this level – and that all the techniques of propaganda implemented within the framework of the Nazi campaigns had, in addition to their authoritarian, autocratic, and hierarchical character, all the characteristics of what Alexander describes in relation to the efforts of mobilization at the time of electoral campaigns, a strong iconography and iconology. We must therefore consider here the ethical dimension correlative to the aesthetic dimension, while marking its ascendancy over the latter – not to mention, of course, the "logic" inherent in the symbolic forms themselves, mobilized on this occasion according to an order that is, for example, "anachronistic," as indicated by the recourse to the Nazi myth in the context of Germany – see, in this respect, Ernst Cassirer (1946).

12 "Counter-performance" does not mean a performance that fails but a performance that is situated in response to another; it is

thus the game of responses between performance and counter-performance which is considered here, and in both cases the "public" is able to assess whether the meaning corresponds to expectations.

13 It is of course worth remembering that the Bush administration's "response," after its initial successes with US (and international) public opinion, did not generate much support for its cause beyond a principled challenge to terrorism, since its own war activities were plagued by serious problems of credibility and legitimacy – as demonstrated by Secretary of State Colin Powell's "performance" before the UN Security Council in February 2003 (Alexander 2011a: 189–90).

14 It is at the juncture of the aesthetic and the political that this occurs. See, on this topic, Alexander 2011c, 2010c and 2008.

15 As they write: "Actors have iconic awareness when they experience material objects, not only by understanding them cognitively or evaluating them morally, but also feeling their sensual, aesthetic force" (Alexander, Bartmański, and Giesen 2012: 1).

16 Alexander reproaches Peirce for confusing the symbolic nature of the icon with simple individualized or objectal representation (Alexander 2006: 649, n. 76). He would rather valorize the properly symbolic nature of the icon (which, in a Peircian register, amounts either to distorting the universal character of the symbol or to betraying the simple representational nature of the icon). For Alexander, Peirce thus privileges science, according to a realist perspective, in its capacity to express "laws" associated with the symbolic to the detriment of aesthetics, and which are associated with representation alone (Alexander 2010c). One could, however, point out in this respect that it is precisely this play of symbolization that illustrates the dialectic of the power in question.

17 The role of the media in this context is not to be overlooked, as Alexander himself shows when he refers to the way in which *Time* magazine, by putting Martin Luther King on the front cover in January 1957, contributed to "making this symbol an icon" (Alexander 2006: 314).

18 Alexander writes:

> Iconic awareness occurs when an aesthetically shaped materiality signifies social value. Contact with this aesthetic surface, whether by sight, smell, taste, sound or touch, provides a sensual experience that transmits meaning. The iconic is about experience, not communication. To be iconically conscious is to understand without knowing, or at least without knowing that

one knows. It is to understand by feeling, by contact, by the "evidence of the senses" rather than by the mind. (2010c: 11)

Even though Freud is mentioned in this context, one realizes, however, that nowhere in Alexander's work is the notion of the unconscious to be found, and that any further elaboration on this front (in relation to, say, the conflict inherent in the relationship between drives and symbolic representations) is excluded from consideration.

19 Warhol's formula that, "in the future, everyone will be world famous for 15 minutes" is of course well known because of its popularization, but its highly ironic content, which highlights the ephemeral nature of fame in a mass democratic society whose fundamental principle is advertising in its relationship to immediate consumption, is dismissed by Alexander in his observation of the durability of certain iconic figures.

20 I have noted, in another context, the limitations of Alexander's position on the theatricality of social life, particularly in relation to the expression of the contemporary theatrical avant-garde and what it reveals to us about the deep symbolic structures of the contemporary social order (Côté 2021).

21 In a methodological note in his book *What Makes a Social Crisis? The Societalization of Social Problems* (2019), Alexander writes:

Because in so constructing events mass media are highly attentive to the sensibilities of those who consume their reports – the audiences of individuals who form their own understandings of contentious social processes as the latter unfold – media reports provide a privileged access to the collective consciousness. It is via competing efforts at public narrative that social meanings are produced, social structures and spheres crystallized and activated, and efficient causation established. Such narrative efforts are reported on by mainstream news outlets that, at the same time, have a major role in the construction of the narratives: they not only report facts that have happened but evaluate ongoing events in terms of their own values and elitist interests, thus creating new facts and new narrations. Only by tracing representations of "events" can we discover the sociologically powerful (because publicly binding) interpretations that provide evidentiary claims of this study. (2019: 119, n. 1)

22 It may be added here that Alexander's spontaneous sympathy for the journalistic profession was established through his own life path, marked initially by a personal experience in the 1960s–1970s in which the choice between sociology and

journalism came to him – as he mentions in an interview with Frédéric Vandenberghe (2019).

Conclusion

1 This does not, of course, exclude research in the broader field of cultural sociology, as evidenced by the two journals *Cultural Sociology* and the *American Journal of Cultural Sociology*, as mentioned in the introduction to this book, as well as the compendiums published and the many authors who are now part of this current.

2 See Alexander and Tognato, *The Civil Sphere in Latin America* (2018); Alexander, Palmer, Park, and Shuk-mei Ku, *The Civil Sphere in East Asia* (2019); Alexander, Lund, and Voyer, *The Nordic Civil Sphere* (2019), and Alexander, Kivisto, and Sciortino, *Populism in the Civil Sphere* (2021). Further co-edited volumes presenting the cases for the civil sphere in India and Canada are now in preparation.

3 It is really along these lines that this movement of analysis of civil society has developed on an international level – see in particular Alexander's "The Arc of Civil Liberation: Obama – Tahrir – Occupy" (2013b). On one aspect of this question of the modalities of integration into the civil sphere in Europe, see in particular Alexander's "Struggling over the Mode of Incorporation: Backlash against Multiculturalism in Europe" (2013c).

4 In saying this, I do not exclude the questions raised today in other fields, such as by the "environmental crisis," which also call for radical transformations of the symbolic structures underlying many of our common conceptions, endorsed at a time when environmental awareness was not what it has become today. See among others Smith and Howe (2015).

5 In response to criticisms of his book *The Civil Sphere* by a few authors (including Robert N. Bellah, Bryan S. Turner, and Axel Honneth), Alexander offers nine theses related to his conceptualization that include the elements listed here – see Alexander, "Nine Theses on the Civil Sphere" (2015).

References

Alexander, J. C. (1982a) *Theoretical Logic in Sociology*, vol. 1: *Positivism, Presuppositions, and Current Controversies*. Berkeley: University of California Press.

— (1982b) *Theoretical Logic in Sociology*, vol. 2: *The Antinomies of Classical Thought: Marx and Durkheim*. Berkeley: University of California Press.

— (1983a) *Theoretical Logic in Sociology*, vol. 3: *The Classical Attempt at Theoretical Synthesis: Max Weber*. Berkeley: University of California Press.

— (1983b) *Theoretical Logic in Sociology*, vol. 4: *The Modern Reconstruction of Classical Thought: Talcott Parsons*. Berkeley: University of California Press.

—, ed. (1985a) *Neofunctionalism*. New York: Sage.

— (1985b) "Habermas's New Critical Theory: Its Promise and Problems," *American Journal of Sociology*, 91(2): 400–24.

— (1986a) "Rethinking Durkheim's Intellectual Development, I: On Marxism and the Anxiety of Being Misunderstood," *International Sociology*, 1(1): 91–107.

— (1986b) "Rethinking Durkheim's Intellectual Development, II: Working Out a Religious Sociology," *International Sociology*, 1(2): 189–201.

— (1987) *Twenty Lectures: Sociological Theory since World War II*. New York: Columbia University Press.

—, ed. (1988a) *Durkheimian Sociology: Cultural Studies*. Cambridge: Cambridge University Press.

— (1988b) "Culture and Political Crisis: 'Watergate' and

Durkheimian Sociology," in J. C. Alexander, ed., *Durkheimian Sociology: Cultural Studies.* Cambridge: Cambridge University Press, pp. 187–224.

— (1989) *Structure and Meaning: Rethinking Classical Sociology.* New York: Columbia University Press.

— (1990) "Introduction: Understanding the 'Relative Autonomy of Culture,'" in J. C. Alexander and S. Seidman, eds, *Culture and Society: Contemporary Debates.* Cambridge: Cambridge University Press, pp. 1–27.

— (1991a) "Bringing Democracy Back In: Universalistic Solidarity and the Civil Sphere," in C. C. Lemert, ed., *Intellectuals and Politics: Social Theory in a Changing World.* London: Sage, pp. 157–76.

— (1991b) "Sociological Theory and the Claim to Reason: Why the End is Not in Sight," *Sociological Theory*, 9(2): 147–53.

— (1992a) "Citizen and Enemy as Symbolic Classification: On the Polarizing Discourse of Civil Society," in M. Lamont and M. Fournier, eds, *Cultivating Differences: Symbolic Boundaries and the Making of Inequality.* Chicago: University of Chicago Press, pp. 289–308.

— (1992b) "General Theory in the Postpositivist Mode: The 'Epistemological Dilemma' and the Search for Present Reason," in S. Seidman and D. G. Wagner, eds, *Postmodernism and Social Theory.* London: Blackwell, pp. 322–68.

— (1995) *Fin de siècle Social Theory: Relativism, Reduction, and the Problem of Reason.* London: Verso.

— (1996a) "Cultural Sociology or Sociology of Culture? Towards a Strong Program," *Culture*, 10(3): 1, 3–5.

— (1996b) "Collective Action, Culture and Civil Society: Secularizing, Updating, Revising and Displacing the Classical Model of Social Movements," in J. Clark and M. Diani, eds, *Alain Touraine.* New York: Routledge, pp. 205–34.

— (1997) "The Paradoxes of Civil Society," *International Sociology*, 12(2): 115–16.

— (1998a) "Civil Societies between Difference and Solidarity: Rethinking Integration in the Fragmented Public Sphere," *Theoria: A Journal of Social and Political Theory*, 92: 1–14.

— (1998b) *Neofunctionalism and After.* Oxford: Blackwell.

— (1999) "Why We All Might Be Able to Live Together: An Immanent Critique of Alain Touraine's *Pourrons-nous vivre ensemble?*," *Thesis Eleven*, 58: 99–105.

— (2000) "Theorizing the Good Society: Hermeneutic, Normative and Empirical Discourses," *Canadian Journal of Sociology*, 25(3): 271–309.

— (2001) "The Binary Discourse of Civil Society," in S. Seidman and J. C. Alexander, eds, *The New Social Theory Reader.* London: Routledge, pp. 193–201.

— (2003) *The Meanings of Social Life: A Cultural Sociology.* Oxford: Oxford University Press.

— (2004a) "Cultural Pragmatics: Social Performance Between Ritual and Strategy," *Sociological Theory*, 22(4): 527–73.

— (2004b) "From the Depths of Despair: Performance, Counter-Performance, and 'September 11,'" *Sociological Theory*, 22(1): 88–105.

— (2004c) "Rethinking Strangeness: From Structures in Space to Discourses in Civil Society," *Thesis Eleven*, 79: 87–104.

— (2005a) "Contradictions in the Societal Community: The Promise and Disappointment of Parsons's Concept," in R. C. Fox, V. M. Lidz and H. J. Bershady, eds, *After Parsons: A Theory of Social Action for the Twenty-First Century.* New York: Russell Sage Foundation, pp. 93–110.

— (2005b) "The Sixties and Me: From Cultural Revolution to Cultural Theory," in A. Sica and S. Turner, eds, *The Disobedient Generation: Social Theorists in the Sixties.* Chicago: University of Chicago Press, pp. 37–47.

— (2006) *The Civil Sphere.* Oxford: Oxford University Press.

— (2008) "Clifford Geertz and the Strong Program: The Human Sciences and Cultural Sociology," *Cultural Sociology*, 2(2): 157–68.

— (2010a) *The Performance of Politics: Obama's Victory and the Democratic Struggle for Power.* Oxford: Oxford University Press.

— (2010b) "The Celebrity Icon," *Cultural Sociology*, 4(3): 323–36.

— (2010c) "Heroes, Presidents, and Politics," *Contexts*, 4(9): 16–21.

— (2011a) *Performance and Power.* Cambridge: Polity.

— (2011b) *Performative Revolution in Egypt: An Essay in Cultural Power.* London: Bloomsbury Academic.

— (2011c) "Fact-Signs and Cultural Sociology: How Meaning-Making Liberates the Social Imagination," *Thesis Eleven*, 104: 87–93.

— (2012a) *Trauma: A Social Theory.* Cambridge: Polity.

— (2012b) "Iconic Power and Performance: The Role of the Critic," in J. C. Alexander, D. Bartmański and B. Giesen, eds, *Iconic Power: Materiality and Meaning in Social Life.* New York: Palgrave Macmillan, pp. 25–35.

— (2013a) *The Dark Side of Modernity.* Cambridge: Polity.

— (2013b) "The Arc of Civil Liberation: Obama – Tahrir – Occupy," *Philosophy and Social Criticism*, 39(4–5): 341–7.

— (2013c) "Struggling over the Mode of Incorporation: Backlash against Multiculturalism in Europe," *Ethnic and Racial Studies*, 36(4): 531–56.

— (2014a) "The Fate of the Dramatic in Modern Society: Social Theory and the Theatrical Avant-Garde," *Theory, Culture and Society*, 31(1): 3–24.

— (2014b) "In Memoriam: Robert Neelly Bellah (23 February, 1927–30 July, 2013)," *American Journal of Cultural Sociology*, 2(1–2): 1.

— (2015) "Nine Theses on the Civil Sphere," in P. Kivisto and G. Sciortino, eds, *Solidarity, Justice, and Incorporation: Thinking through* The Civil Sphere, Oxford: Oxford University Press, pp. 172–90.

— (2017a) *The Drama of Social Life*. Cambridge: Polity.

— (2017b) "Raging against the Enlightenment: The Ideology of Steven Bannon," *ASA Sociology of Culture Newsletter*, 29(12): 24–8.

— (2018a) "Frontlash/Backlash: The Crisis of Solidarity and the Threat to Civil Institutions," *Contemporary Sociology: A Journal Review*, 48(1): 5–11.

— (2018b) "La théorie anti-utilitariste de Parsons à Durkheim et à l'actuelle sociologie culturelle," in A. Caillé, P. Chanial, S. Dufoix and F. Vandenberghe, *Des sciences sociales à la science sociale: fondements anti-utilitaristes*. Lormont: Le Bord de l'eau, pp. 185–9.

— (2019) *What Makes a Social Crisis? The Societalization of Social Problems*. Cambridge: Polity.

Alexander, J. C., and Colomy, P. (1985) "Toward Neofunctionalism," *Sociological Theory*, 3(2): 11–23.

— (1990) "Neofunctionalism Today: Reconstructing a Theoretical Tradition," in G. Ritzer, ed., *Frontiers of Social Theory: The New Synthesis*. New York: Columbia University Press, pp. 33–67.

Alexander, J. C., and Jaworski, B. N. (2014) *Obama Power*. Cambridge: Polity.

Alexander, J. C., and Mast, J. L. (2006) "Introduction: Symbolic Action in Theory and Practice: the Cultural Pragmatics of Symbolic Action," in J. C. Alexander, B. Giesen and J. L. Mast, eds, *Social Performance: Symbolic Action, Cultural Pragmatics, and Ritual*. Cambridge: Cambridge University Press, pp. 1–28.

Alexander, J. C., and Sherwood, S. J. (2002) "'Mythic Gestures': Robert N. Bellah and Cultural Sociology," in R. Madsen, W. M. Sullivan, A. Swidler and S. M. Tipton, eds, *Meaning and Modernity*. Berkeley: University of California Press, pp. 1–14.

Alexander, J. C., and Smith, P. (1993) "The Discourse of American

Civil Society: A New Proposal for Cultural Studies," *Theory and Society*, 22(2): 151–207.

— (1998) "Sociologie culturelle ou sociologie de la culture? Un programme fort pour donner à la sociologie son second souffle," *Sociologie and Sociétés*, 30(1): 1–10.

— (2002) "The Strong Program in Cultural Theory: Elements of a Structural Hermeneutics," in J. Turner, ed., *Handbook of Sociological Theory*. New York: Kluwer Academic/Plenum, pp. 135–50.

—, eds (2005) *The Cambridge Companion to Durkheim*. Cambridge: Cambridge University Press.

Alexander, J. C., and Tognato, C., eds (2018) *The Civil Sphere in Latin America*. Cambridge: Polity.

Alexander, J. C., Eyerman, R., Giesen, B., Smelser, N. J., and Sztompka, P., eds (2004) *Cultural Trauma and Collective Identity*. Berkeley: University of California Press.

Alexander, J. C, Giesen, B., and Mast, J. L., eds (2006) *Social Performance: Symbolic Action, Cultural Pragmatics, and Ritual*. Cambridge: Cambridge University Press.

Alexander, J. C., Bartmański, D., and Giesen, B., eds (2012) *Iconic Power: Materiality and Meaning in Social Life*. New York: Palgrave Macmillan.

Alexander, J. C., Jacobs, R. N., and Smith, P. (2012) *The Oxford Handbook of Cultural Sociology*. Oxford: Oxford University Press.

Alexander, J. C., Butler Breeze, E., and Luengo, M., eds (2016) *The Crisis of Journalism Reconsidered*. Cambridge: Cambridge University Press.

Alexander, J. C., Lund, A., and Voyer, A., eds (2019) *The Nordic Civil Sphere*. Cambridge: Polity.

Alexander, J. C., Palmer, D. A., Park, S., and Shuk-Mei Ku, A., eds (2019) *The Civil Sphere in East Asia*. Cambridge: Polity.

Alexander, J. C., Kivisto, P., and Sciortino, G., eds (2021) *Populism in the Civil Sphere*. Cambridge: Polity.

Bakhtin, M. M. (1982) *The Dialogic Imagination: Four Essays*, trans. M. Holquist and C. Emerson. Austin: University of Texas Press.

Barnes, B. (1974) *Scientific Knowledge and Sociological Theory*. London: Routledge.

Barthes, R. (2013) *Mythologies*, trans. R. Howard. New York: Hill & Wang.

Bell, D. (1976) *The Cultural Contradictions of Capitalism*. New York: Basic Books.

Bellah, R. N. (1978) *The Broken Covenant: American Civil Religion in Time of Trial*. Chicago: University of Chicago Press.

Bellah, R. N., Madsen, R., Sullivan, W. M., Swidler, A., and Tipton, S. M. (1985) *Habits of the Heart*. Berkeley: University of California Press.

Bellah, R. N., Madsen, R., Sullivan, W. N., and Tipton, S. M. (1992) *The Good Society*. New York: Vintage Books.

Blau, P. M. (1975) *Approaches to the Study of Social Structure*. New York: Free Press.

Bloor, D. (1991) *Knowledge and Social Imagery*. Chicago: University of Chicago Press.

Blumer, H. (1969) *Symbolic Interactionism: Perspective and Method*. Englewood Cliffs, NJ: Prentice Hall.

Bourdieu, P. (1988) *L'ontologie politique de Martin Heidegger*. Paris: Éditions de Minuit.

Buxton, W. (1985) *Talcott Parsons and the Capitalist Nation-State*. Toronto: University of Toronto Press.

Caillé, A. (1981) "La sociologie de l'intérêt, est-elle intéressante? À propos de l'utilisation du paradigme de l'économie en sociologie," *Sociologie du travail*, 3(3): 257–74.

Caillé, A. and Vandenberghe, F. (2016) *Pour une nouvelle sociologie classique*. Lormont: Le Bord de l'eau.

Cassirer, E. (1944) *Essay on Man*. New Haven, CT: Yale University Press.

— (1946) *The Myth of the State*. New Haven, CT: Yale University Press.

— (2000) *The Logic of the Cultural Sciences*, trans. S. G. Lofts. New Haven, CT: Yale University Press.

Cefaï, D. (2007) *Pourquoi se mobilise-t-on? Les théories de l'action collective*. Paris, La Découverte/MAUSS.

Coleman, J. C. (1960) *Personality Dynamics and Effective Behavior*. Chicago: Foresman Scott.

Cordero, R., Carballo, F., and Ossandón, J. (2008) "Performing Cultural Sociology: A Conversation with Jeffrey Alexander," *European Journal of Social Theory*, 11(4): 523–42.

Côté, J.-F. (2011) "Persona, skènè, drama: la grande transformation du théâtre et de la sociologie," *Cahiers de recherche sociologique*, 51: 97–114.

— (2015) *George Herbert Mead's Concept of Society: A Critical Reconstruction*. New York: Routledge.

— (2021) "Bridging Cultural Sociology with Francophone Sociologists: A Transcultural Challenge," *American Journal of Cultural Sociology*, 9(4): 581–99.

Dilthey, W. (2010) *Understanding the Human World*, in *Selected Works*, vol. II, ed. R. A. Makkrel and F. Rodi. Princeton, NJ: Princeton University Press.

Durkheim, E. ([1912] 1963) *The Elementary Forms of Religious Life*, trans. K. E. Fields. New York: Free Press.

Durkheim, E., and Mauss, M. ([1903] 1963) *Primitive Classification*, trans. R. Needham. Chicago: University of Chicago Press.

Eyerman, R., Alexander, J. C., and Butler Breese, E., eds (2011) *Narrating Trauma: On the Impact of Collective Suffering*. New York: Routledge.

Gadamer, H.-G. (1989) *Truth and Method*, trans. J. Wansheimer and D. G. Marshall. London: Bloomsbury.

Garfinkel, H. (1967) *Studies in Ethnomethodology*. Englewood Cliffs, NJ: Prentice Hall.

Geertz, C. (1973) *The Interpretation of Cultures*. New York: Basic Books.

— (1983) *Local Knowledge: Further Essays in Interpretive Anthropology*. New York: Basic Books.

Goffman, E. (1959) *The Presentation of Self in Everyday Life*. New York: Doubleday Anchor Books.

Grossberg, L., Nelson, C., and Treicher, P., eds (1991) *Cultural Studies*. New York: Routledge.

Habermas, J. ([1968] 1987) *Knowledge and Human Interests*, trans. J. J. Shapiro. Cambridge: Polity.

— ([1962] 1989) *The Structural Transformation of the Public Sphere*, trans. Thomas Burger and Frederick Lawrence. Cambridge: Polity.

Hall, J. R., Grindstaff, L., and Lo, M.-C., eds (2012) *Handbook of Cultural Sociology*. New York: Routledge.

Hall, S. ([1973] 2021) "Encoding and Decoding in the Television Discourse," in *Writings on Media: History in the Present*. Durham, NC: Duke University Press, pp. 247–66.

Hegel, G. W. F. (1991) *Elements of the Philosophy of Right*. Cambridge: Cambridge University Press.

Hobbes, T. ([1651] 2006) *Leviathan*. Oxford: Oxford University Press.

Inglis, D., and Almila, A.-M., eds (2016) *The Sage Handbook of Cultural Sociology*. London: Sage.

Inglis, D., Blaikie, A., and Wagner-Pacifici, R. (2007) "Editorial: Sociology, Culture and the 21st Century," *Cultural Sociology*, 1(1): 1–18.

Jakobson, R. (2010) "Linguistics and Communication Theory," in *Selected Writings*, vol. II: *Word and Language*. Berlin: Mouton de Gruyter, pp. 570–7.

Joas, H. (1985) *G. H. Mead: A Contemporary Re-examination of His Thought*, trans. R. Meyer. Cambridge, MA: MIT Press.

Kurasawa, F. (2004) "Alexander and the Refounding of American Sociology," *Thesis Eleven*, 79: 53–64.

Lamont, M. (1998) "Book Review: *Fin de siècle Social Theory: Relativism, Reduction, and the Problem of Reason,*" *American Journal of Sociology*, 103(4): 1068–9.

Lamont, M., and Fournier, M. (1992) *Cultivating Differences: Symbolic Boundaries and the Making of Inequality*. Chicago: University of Chicago Press.

Lamont, M., and Wuthnow, R. (1990) "Betwixt and Between: Recent Cultural Sociology in Europe and the United States," in G. Ritzer, ed., *Frontiers of Social Theory: The New Synthesis*. New York: Columbia University Press, pp. 287–315.

Loader, C., and Alexander, J. C. (1985) "Max Weber on Churches and Sects in North America: An Alternative Path toward Rationalization," *Sociological Theory*, 3(1): 1–6.

Mannheim, K. (1954) *Ideology and Utopia: An Introduction to the Sociology of Knowledge*, trans. L. Wirth and E. Shils. New York: Harcourt, Brace.

Marshall, A. (1890) *Principles of Economics*. London: Macmillan.

Mauss, M. (1989) "Une catégorie de l'esprit humain: la notion de personne, celle de 'moi,'" in *Sociologie et anthropologie*. Paris: Presses universitaires de France, pp. 331–62.

— (2000) *The Gift: The Form and Reason for Exchange in Archaic Society*. New York: W. W. Norton.

McLennan, G. (2005) "The 'New American Cultural Sociology': An Appraisal," *Theory, Culture & Society*, 22(6): 1–18.

Mead, G. H. (1934) *Mind, Self and Society*. Chicago: University of Chicago Press.

— (1936) *Movements of Thought in the Nineteenth Century*. Chicago: University of Chicago Press.

Miller, P. (1964) *Errand into the Wilderness*. New York: Harper Torchbooks.

Parsons, T. (1951) *The Social System*. New York: Free Press.

— (1966) *Societies: Evolutionary and Comparative Perspectives*. Englewood Cliffs, NJ: Prentice Hall.

— ([1937] 1968) *The Structure of Social Action*, 2 vols. New York: Free Press.

— (1971) *The System of Modern Societies*. Englewood Cliffs, NJ: Prentice Hall.

— (2007) *American Society: A Theory of the Societal Community*, ed. G. Sciortino. Boulder, CO: Paradigm.

Pizarro-Noël, F. (2014) "The Two Durkheims of Parsons and Alexander," *Cahiers de recherche sociologique*, 56: 87–108.

Ricœur, P. (1965) *De l'interprétation: essai sur Freud*. Paris: Éditions du Seuil.

Roberge, J. (2009) "Jeffrey C. Alexander et les dix ans du programme fort en sociologie culturelle," *Cahiers de recherche sociologique*, no. 47: 47–66.

Schechner, R. (2003) *Performance Theory*. New York: Routledge.

Schütz, A. (1967) *The Phenomenology of the Social World*, trans. G. Walsh and F. Lehnert. Evanston, IL: Northwestern University Press.

Sherwood, S. J., Smith, P., and Alexander, J. C. (1993) "The British Are Coming ... Again! The Hidden Agenda of 'Cultural Studies'?," *Contemporary Sociology*, 22(3): 370–5.

Smith, P., ed. (1998) *The New American Cultural Sociology*. Cambridge: Cambridge University Press.

— (2005) *Why War? The Cultural Logic of Iraq, the Gulf War and Suez*. Chicago: University of Chicago Press.

Smith, P., and Howe, N. (2015) *Climate Change as Social Drama*. Cambridge: Cambridge University Press.

Strauss, A., ed. (1956) *George Herbert Mead on Social Psychology*. Chicago: University of Chicago Press.

Tocqueville, A. de ([1835] 2004) *Democracy in America*, trans. A. Goldhammer. New York: Library of America.

Touraine, A. (1992) *Critique de la modernité*. Paris: Fayard.

— (1994) *Qu'est-ce que la démocratie?* Paris: Fayard.

Tracy, D. de (1970) *Éléments d'idéologie*. Paris: Vrin.

Turner, S. (1985) "Book Review: *Theoretical Logic in Sociology*, vol. 1: *Positivism, Presuppositions, and Current Controversies*," *Philosophy of the Social Sciences*, 15(1): 77–82.

Turner, V. (1982) *From Ritual to Theatre: The Human Seriousness of Play*. Ann Arbor: University of Michigan Press.

Vandenberghe, F. (2000) "Introduction à la logique théorique de Jeffrey C. Alexander," in Alexander, *La réduction: critique de Bourdieu*. Paris: Éditions du Cerf, pp. 9–18.

— (2019) "From Journalism to Cultural Sociology (and Back via Parsons): An Interview with Jeffrey Alexander," *Sociologia & Antropologia*, 9(1): 15–40.

Vattimo, G. (1991) *Éthique de l'interprétation*, trans. J. Rolland. Paris: La Découverte.

Voloshinov, V. N. (1986) *Marxism and the Philosophy of Language*, trans. L. Matejka and I. R. Titunik. Cambridge, MA: Harvard University Press.

Weber, M. (1978) *Economy and Society*, vol. I, trans. G. Roth and C. Wittich. Berkeley: University of California Press.

— ([1906] 2003) "Églises et sectes en Amérique du nord," in *L'Éthique protestante et l'esprit du capitalisme*, trans. J. P. Grossein. Paris: Flammarion, pp. 257–77.

— (2017) *The Protestant Work Ethic and the Spirit of Capitalism*, trans. T. Parsons. New York: Vigo Press.

Index

Main references are listed in bold.

Durkheim, Émile 6, 10, 13,
16, 17, 18, 19, 23, 25, 29,
30–7, 38, 39, 42, 44, 45,
46, 50, 60, 62, 63, 65, 66,
69, 71, 73, 74, 76, 81, 82,
89, 104, 118, 122 n1, 126
n20, 129 n1, 130 n3, 130
n5, 130 n6, 130 n7, 133
n1, 136 n1, 138 n8, 140
n12, 144 n5, 145 n6
Durkheimian sociology 2, 18,
22, 26, 31, 37, 42, 132 n15

Eisenstadt, Shmuel N. 20, 21,
79, 118, 127 n23
Elias, Norbert 55
empirical 3, 4, 6, 12, 13, 14,
15, 17, 20, 21, 22, 31, 32,
37, 42, 44, 50, 69, 70, 71,
77, 82, 84, 86, 102, 118,
140 n13
epistemology 25
epistemological 1, 4, 5, 6,
9, 13, 14, 16, 18, 30, 40,
41, 46, 50, 70, 80, 81, 82,
118, 125 n14, 137 n3, 139
n9, 141 n17, 143 n25
onto-epistemological, 118 n14
Eyerman, Ron 58, 97, 126 n19

Fauconnet, Paul 36
Felt, Mark 39
feminism 88, **90–2**, 98
Feuerbach, Ludwig 48
Foucault, Michel 11, 54, 123
n2
Freud, Sigmund 43, 55, 82,
139 n9, 155 n18

Gadamer, Hans-Georg 78, 95,
118, 119, 128 n27, 130 n4,
143 n25, 144 n3
Garfinkel, Harold 17, 71, 83,
140 n13, 140 n14

Geertz, Clifford 6, 12, 25, 26,
44, 72, 73, 74, 79, 83, 118,
123 n3, 127 n23, 127 n25,
132 n15, 134 n8, 149 n22
Giesen, Bernhard 111, 143 n1,
154 n15
Goffman, Erving 71, 140 n12,
151 n4
Gramsci, Antonio 49
Grant, Ulysses S. 76

Habermas, Jürgen 4, 14, 24,
49, **56–60**, 77, 121, 124
n7, 125 n12, 135 n15, 138
n8, 145 n10, 147 n12, 147
n16
Halbwachs, Maurice 36
Hall, John R. 2, 23
Hall, Stuart 3, 51, 134 n7
Hegel, Georg Wilhelm Friedrich
15, 27, 28, 47, 48, 57, 60,
73, 75, 77, 92, 124 n7, 124
n8, 128 n27, 128 n29, 133
n3, 133 n4, 137 n2, 141
n16, 142 n20, 146 n12,
148 n21
hermeneutic 3, 4, 7, 8, 10, 12,
26, 28, 30, 31, 32, 36, 39,
40, 42, 43, 44, 45, 60, 70,
72, 73, 74, 76, 78, 80, 81,
88, 93, 94, 95, 106, 112,
114, 118, 119, 127 n25,
128 n26, 130 n4, 131 n8,
134 n4, 136 n1, 137 n2,
139 n9, 141 n17, 143 n25,
148 n17, 152 n6
Hobbes, Thomas 16, 77
Hoggart, Richard 3, 50, 134
n8
Holocaust 78, 90, **98–9**, 148
n21, 150 n28, 153 n11
Holton, Gerald 14
Honneth, Axel 5, 60, 147 n13,
156 n5

political institution 38, 39,
47, 56, 58, 74, 104
political mobilizations 4,
103, 120
political power 39, 56, 58,
109, 110, 142 n22
political representations 5,
57, 58, 104, 111
postmodern 26, 40, 44, 58, 61,
85, 100, 111, 142 n20
post-positivist **13–18**, 21, 24–6,
56, 77, 80, 81
power 5, 11, 20, 21, 38, 39,
41, 43, 44, 50, 51, 52, 55,
56, 58, 60, 67, 75, 86, 89,
93, 94, 100, **101–16**, 123
n2, 130 n7, 134 n8, 142
n22, 146 n11, 147 n16,
154 n16, 155 n21
pragmatism 42, 54, 60, 61, 70,
72, 126 n29, 131 n9, 134
n9, 135 n12, 136 n15, 140
n11, 140 n13, 140 n15
pragmatic 3, 5, 23, 26, 70,
93, 96, 97, 105, 150 n26
profane 7, 31, 33, 34, 37–44,
92, 119, 129 n3, 131 n11,
150 n25
psychoanalysis 43, 82, 98, 111
psychoanalytic 6, 98,

reason 28, 47, 57, 59, 60, 61,
63, 78, 128 n27, 128 n29,
135 n10, 136 n15, 137 n3,
143 n25, 143 n26
reflexivity 2, 6, 8, 9, **25–9**, 42,
48, 49, 52, 54, 55, **56–61**,
80, 81, 85, 91, 101, 107,
114, 116, 134, 150 n25
religion 5, 7, 31, 33–7, 42,
45–9, 57, 61, 62–7, 73, 74,
81, 86, 90, 104, 106, 108,
112, 129 n3, 130 n6, 133
n4, 139 n9, 141 n19, 145

n6, 147 n16, 148 n18, 149
n22, 151 n1
civil religion 28, 39, 62, 64,
69, **74–8**, 81, 95, 104, 108,
129 n3, 142 n20, 149 n22
Rickert, Heinrich 7, 124 n7
Ricœur, Paul 43, 72, 78, 128
n27, 134 n4, 139 n9
ritual 3, 24, 30, 32, 34, 38, 39,
40, 44, 52, 71, 81, 93, 97,
104, 105, 107, 113, 114,
130 n2, 134 n7, 140 n12,
145 n6
ritualization 4

sacred 7, 31, 33, 34–41, 44, 89,
92, 106, 111, 119, 129 n3,
130 n6, 130 n7, 131 n11
Sartre, Jean-Paul 49
Saussure, Ferdinand de 7, 41,
73, 95, 131 n9, 149 n24
Schechner, Richard 6, 93, 113,
149 n22
Schütz, Alfred 17, 71, 139 n10
semiology 3, 6, 7, 131 n9
semiotic 5, 26, 39, 41, 45, 51,
60, 76, 111, 123 n4, 129
n3, 131 n9, 132 n14, 134
n7, 140 n13, 149 n24
Sherwood, Steven Jay 50, 52,
74, 134 n8
Shils, Edward 79
Simmel, Georg 7, 136 n2
Smelser, Neil 13, 79, 127 n23
Smith, Philip 2, 3, 5, 10, 11,
12, 23, 24, 25, 50, 57, 76,
88, 126 n19, 126 n20, 130
n3, 131 n11, 143 n24, 143
n1, 144 n4, 156 n4
Smith, Robertson 33
social movements 58, 61, 77,
87, **88–92**, 98, 121, 147
n14, 148 n18
Spencer, Herbert 19